HOW
COME,
GOD?

Other books by David M. Howard

Hammered As Gold
Student Power in World Evangelism

DAVID M. HOWARD

HOW COME, GOD?

Reflections from Job
about God and Puzzled Man

A. J. HOLMAN COMPANY
Division of J. B. Lippincott Company
Philadelphia and New York

U.S. Library of Congress Cataloging in Publication Data

Howard, David M
  How come, God?

  1. Bible. O. T. Job—Criticism, interpretation, etc. 2.
Providence and government of God—Biblical teaching. I.
Title.
BS1415.2.H67   223'.1'066   72-3477
ISBN-0-87981-010-6

To my children

DAVID, STEPHEN, KAREN ELISABETH,
AND MICHAEL

*My prayer for them is that they,
like Job, should be blameless, upright,
fearing God, and turning away from evil.*

CONTENTS

Foreword by Joseph Bayley   9
Preface   11
Acknowledgments   13

I.   "The Lord Gave, and the Lord Has Taken Away"
    (Introduction to Job)   17

II.   "My Servant Job"
    (Prologue, chs. 1, 2)   22

III.   "Oh, That I Knew Where I Might Find Him"
    (Job, ch. 3 et al.)   30

IV.   "Who That Was Innocent Ever Perished?"
    (Eliphaz, chs. 4, 5)   41

V.   "Have You Listened in the Council of God?"
    (Eliphaz, chs. 15, 22)   48

VI.   "Inquire . . . of Bygone Ages"
    (Bildad, chs. 8, 18, 25)   56

VII.   "Less Than Your Guilt Deserves"
    (Zophar, chs. 11, 20)   62

VIII.   "The Outskirts of His Ways"
    (Job, chs. 13, 26)   65

IX.   "When the Friendship of God Was Upon My Tent"
    (Job, chs. 26, 27, 29–31)   71

X. "Where Shall Wisdom Be Found?"
(Job, ch. 28) — 79

XI. "When He Is Quiet, Who Can Condemn?"
(Elihu, chs. 32–35) — 85

XII. "For Love, He Causes It to Happen"
(Elihu, chs. 36, 37) — 95

XIII. "Where Were You . . . ?"
(Jehovah, chs. 38–41) — 102

XIV. "Now My Eye Sees Thee"
(Epilogue, ch. 42) — 108

XV. "And After This Job Lived . . ."
(Conclusion) — 115

FOREWORD

Job is an old friend of mine. So is David Howard. I welcome this book for it helps me understand each of them better.

Good Bible exposition is like that: it reveals the revealer, or else it falls flat on the hard concrete of truisms and clichés and dreary repetition. There is much Bible exposition that contracts rather than expands. The great becomes manageable.

The author of this book never quite brings Job under control, nor, do I suspect, does he intend to. It is enough to show the magnitude of the man who knew God, even though he didn't know the answers to all his questions.

But who does? Who has never said, "Why me? Why doesn't God do something about this? How can God allow it?" only to find the heavens silent, although his friends may have words to speak?

I think that the experiences of David Howard's life and walk with God authenticate his ideas and qualify him to write about Job. This book is full of those experiences — the drowning of a promising student at an Inter-Varsity camp in Costa Rica for which David Howard was responsible; crises in the Colombia work which he headed; the suffering and death of missionary-statesman Kenneth Strachan; a close friend's violent assassination by mountain bandits. And in the background is the death of his five friends at the hands of savage Aucas.

The author's father, Philip E. Howard, Jr., once wrote that a night of sleeplessness because of pain will do more to bring a man close to God than many years of ordinary living. C. S. Lewis called pain "God's megaphone to rouse a deaf world."

I think this book, like the Book of Job, will rouse people and bring them close to God—the God who is not a Super

HOW COME, GOD?

Computer, taking in countless bits of information and spewing forth answers, but the God who is a Father who loves us enough to let us suffer in the night, knowing that daybreak will surely come.

Joseph Bayly
Bartlett, Illinois

PREFACE

Can a man really know God in a personal, vital, and living way, even when he cannot solve all the problems of suffering or of life in general which surround him? These are questions being asked today in the latter part of the twentieth century. They were also asked centuries ago in the Book of Job. For those who desire easy answers to the deep and perplexing problems of life, the Book of Job will be a disappointment, for no answers are given to some questions. But for those who are willing to face these perplexities honestly and openly, and who desire a real and living relationship with God, few books are more exciting than Job.

Job is a complex book with a variety of textual and critical problems which the scholars have never resolved. Its authorship, date, and place of writing are all obscure. It is generally agreed that it is a very ancient book, probably dating from the time of the patriarchs and perhaps written in the land of Edom. Some of the textual difficulties may never be resolved satisfactorily by biblical scholars.

However, Job is a universal poem. Its value lies in the fact that the problems with which Job struggles in his search for a direct relationship with God are universal and relevant to every age and every culture. Therefore, the fact that some critical problems remain unsolved in no way affects the basic message of the book. The fact that some questions remain unanswered gives life and meaning to this message in an age when confusion, calamity, and distress are the order of the day.

To the question posed above, the Book of Job, when studied objectively, comes through with a resounding "*Yes!* Man *can* know God regardless of unanswerable questions!" This is the message that needs to be heard today.

It is not my purpose here to deal with critical or textual problems, even when I am aware of their presence. This is left to more competent scholars. Rather, I hope that the reader may interact with Job as a man who struggled with problems very similar to the ones with which modern man is struggling. The answers offered by his friends sound strangely familiar to modern ears. We have heard them often enough today! It is my hope that this encounter with Job may lead to a deep and abiding encounter with the God of Job, who is the God of eternity, the God of all creation, and the God of love and mercy. If this purpose is reached, I shall be grateful.

ACKNOWLEDGMENTS

Grateful acknowledgment is expressed to the following publishers for permission to quote from copyrighted material:

The Association Press for material from *Two Centuries of Student Christian Movements* by Clarence Shedd, copyright 1943.

David C. Cook Publishing Company for material from *The View from a Hearse* by Joseph Bayly, copyright 1969.

Harper and Row for material from *Who Shall Ascend?* by Elisabeth Elliot, copyright 1968.

Houghton Mifflin Company for Tennyson's poem "In Memoriam" taken from *The Complete Poetical Works of Alfred Tennyson*, copyright 1884.

Marshall, Morgan, and Scott for material from *Baffled to Fight Better* by Oswald Chambers, copyright 1931. (Distributed in U.S.A. by Christian Literature Crusade.)

SCM Press for material from *The Triumph of Job* by Edgar Jones, copyright 1966.

Society for Promoting Christian Knowledge for the poem by Amy Carmichael, "In Acceptance Lieth Peace," from *Toward Jerusalem*, copyright 1936. (Distributed in U.S.A. by Christian Literature Crusade.)

Zondervan Publishing House for material from *Bible Characters* by Alexander Whyte, copyright 1952.

Special thanks are also expressed to the following individuals for permission to quote from their writings:

E. Margaret Clarkson for permission to quote her poem "In Darkness."

Edmund Clowney for permission to quote from his paper "The Sovereignty of God and the Lostness of Man."

The Scripture quotations in this publication are from the Revised Standard Version of the Bible, copyrighted 1946 and 1952 by the Division of Christian Education of the National Council of Churches of Christ in the U.S.A., and used by permission.

I also wish to express deep personal thanks to Molly Fahringer, who typed and edited the original draft and checked all Scripture quotations; to May Koksma, who typed the second draft; and to Kay Barton, who typed the final draft and helped in final editing. Their efficient work provided great satisfaction as the manuscript progressed.

Thanks also go to the publishers and, in particular, to Russell Hitt, editor, for invaluable advice and editorial help.

HOW COME, GOD?

I

"The Lord Gave, and the Lord Has Taken Away"

(Introduction to Job)

"I hate to tell you this, Dave, but we've lost one of the boys down here. Dale Bowman has drowned!" The voice on the other end of the phone was taut with emotion.

"No! This can't be!" was my first reaction. How could it possibly be? I was stunned momentarily into silence. I was directing the first Overseas Training Camp of Inter-Varsity Christian Fellowship being held in San José, Costa Rica. Forty students from the U.S. were with us for a month of intensive exposure to God's work in another land. Dale Bowman was clearly one of the outstanding leaders of the camp. During the second week of camp they were divided into teams and sent out around the country for direct contact with grass roots missionary work. One group was in San Isidro under the leadership of Jackie Cooper, a Southern Baptist missionary. It was Jackie who was talking to me on the phone.

As I tried to stabilize my thoughts after the initial shock, Jackie gave me the details. The entire group of eight had been swimming together on a picnic on the Pacific coast. Shortly after noon the tide had changed and a strong undertow developed. The group left the water, with the exception of Dale, who indicated he was on his way. Several moments later, however, the others realized that Dale was in trouble. Ron Kernaghan, Inter-Varsity staff member, immediately dove in and went directly to Dale, while Jackie and the others ran for a rope. Ron managed to reach Dale and discovered that he was already quite weak from struggling against the tide.

For the next forty-five minutes the two men fought the waves and tide, with Dale soon losing consciousness. Ron held him up in the water, determined not to let him go. However, they had been swept too far out to be reached by a rope, and no boat was available. Jackie and the group on shore were stymied, having done all they could to help. Ron decided in his own mind that he would never let Dale go. When the situation became hopeless, Ron resigned himself to drowning with Dale rather than abandoning him.

Suddenly a large wave struck them and separated the two men. Ron lunged to get back to Dale, but was unable to breast the tide. He caught sight of Dale once more as he bobbed up in the waves some distance from him. Then he was lost from sight, never to be seen again by human eyes. Ron, exhausted from long exertion which went far beyond normal physical capacities, lost all sense of consciousness and does not know to this day what happened. The next thing he remembers is being swept up onto the beach and collapsing. He lay there for half an hour while the others worked to revive him.

As I hung up the phone I tried to evaluate what had happened. Dale was one of the most promising young men I had known in a long time. We first met when he was a student at Trinity Evangelical Divinity School in Deerfield, Ill., preparing to serve the Lord in missionary work. He was providing outstanding leadership in the student body with a strong missions emphasis. He was also a student leader in reaching out to other schools to help them organize active missions groups on their campuses.

Coming from a fine Christian family he had been brought up by parents who loved and honored the Lord. He came to a personal knowledge of Jesus Christ as a young boy in his own home.

Throughout his youth he was active in serving the Lord. He helped to found Rockford Chapel where he taught Sunday school, and was also youth director of the Chapelwood Free Church. At Rockford College, where he received his B.A., he was president of the Inter-Varsity chapter. While working for his M.A. in education at Northern Illinois University he continued active in Inter-Varsity and maintained a consistent witness for the Lord. When he applied to attend the Overseas Training Camp he wrote, "It is my continued desire to have Jesus Christ as Lord of my life."

One of the most difficult tasks I have ever had to perform was to place a long distance phone call from Costa Rica to Rockford, Ill., to advise Dale's parents that God had taken their son home to Himself. The call was delayed, and it was midnight before I contacted them. They were awakened out of sleep to be told this tragic news. The deepness of their grief and the agonizing question of "Why?" were beyond words.

Immediately after breaking this news to Mr. and Mrs. Bowman, I left in a jeep with fellow missionary Bob Bennett for San Isidro. Bob had been with Dale and the others for the week in San Isidro, but had come to San José that day with one of the students who had been taken ill. Bob is a rugged man with great physical stamina. Captain of his college football team, husky defenseman on the ice hockey team, he had the qualities that would have made it quite probable that he could have helped Ron Kernaghan to rescue Dale. Inevitably the question kept coming to his lips, "If *only* I could have been there. . . . *Why* did I have to be away that one day?"

For the next two days Red Cross volunteers, local fisher-men, and scores of people from the surrounding area hunted tirelessly for Dale's body. All efforts were in vain. I spent those two days with Ron and the other students, as we tried to face together what God was saying to us in this unexpected and crushing turn of events. Second guessing was the natural tendency. But little by little we had to come to the conclusion that God was still sovereign and that He does all things well.

My mind went back again and again to a time four years previously when my close colleague, Ernest Fowler, had been murdered in the high Andes of Colombia, a story which has been told elsewhere.[1] At that time God spoke to me particu-larly through Ps. 119:75, *"I know, O Lord, that thy judgments are right, and that in faithfulness thou hast afflicted me."* It was hard to believe that this was part of God's faithfulness, but it had to be so.

The perplexing questions of "Why?" were on everyone's lips. Dale had showed such great promise. His potential for effective service for God was unusually high. His warm spirit and loving attitude permeated all he did. Could he not have had a fruitful life and ministry?

Ron Kernaghan could not help but ask, "Why was Dale taken and I left? Why was it not the other way around? Or why didn't we go down together?" Bob Bennett asked, "Why was I not on hand to help when needed?"

And then the Book of Job began to speak to me again, as it had done so often in recent years when unexplainable failures or defeats had been faced. Here was a man who suffered as few, if any, men beside Christ have ever suffered. The

[1]David M. Howard, *Hammered As Gold.* New York: Harper & Row, 1969.

darkness, the pain, the confusion, the silence of God that surrounded Job as he struggled in agony of soul became very real to us again. Dale was gone. There was nothing we could do about it. Why he was gone was unanswered, but life had to proceed. We still had to trust God and believe that "*he knows the way that I take; when He has tried me, I shall come forth as gold*" *(Job 23:10).*

II

"My Servant, Job"
(Prologue, chs. 1, 2)

What is the message of the Book of Job? If the popular idea that the Book of Job is primarily about suffering is correct, then we must conclude that the book is a failure. No real answer is given to the question of why the righteous suffer.

The problem of suffering is discussed at length, but this is not the primary theme of the book. Rather, suffering is a channel through which the basic issue is brought to the fore. The real problem discussed by Job and his friends is the question of a man's relationship to God. Can a man really know God?

The Book of Job raises the question of innocent suffering as a genuinely relevant issue to discuss the whole nature of the relationship between God and man. Why the righteous suffer is discussed to show how a man can truly relate to God.

The prologue provides the introduction. First, who was Job? The first verse of the book tells us that Job *"was blameless and upright, one who feared God, and turned away from evil."* This immediately destroys the idea, so vociferously propounded by Job's friends, that his suffering was a result of his sin. Not only is Job described this way by the writer, but God Himself used this same terminology when He spoke to Satan about him. *"Have you considered my servant Job, that there is none like him on the earth, a blameless and upright man, who fears God and turns away from evil?"* (1:8).

Even the prophet Ezekiel, writing centuries later, saw Job as one of the most righteous men of the Old Testament period. In speaking of the judgment of God upon the land, Ezekiel said, *"even if these three men, Noah, Daniel, and Job, were in it, they would deliver but their own lives by their righteousness, says the Lord God"* (Ezek. 14:14). In other words, Job was one of the three most righteous men to whom Ezekiel could refer.

Clearly, then, Job's suffering was not a result of his sin. This is not to say that Job was not a sinner. Scripture says that every man is a sinner. But Job was a forgiven sinner who was honestly seeking God. The terrible suffering inflicted upon him was not punishment for rebellion against God.

Next comes the scene in heaven. It is significant to note who spoke first. *"Now there was a day when the sons of God came to present themselves before the Lord, and Satan also came among them. The Lord said to Satan, 'Whence have you come?'"* (1:6,7a).

It is of supreme importance in understanding this book to realize that God was the initiator of the whole drama, not Satan. The story begins in heaven, not on earth. When the problems of Job are discussed on earth by Job and his friends, the scene which had already taken place in heaven is outside their scope of knowledge. Yet it is this scene which sets the tone for the book. God and Satan had already discussed Job, but Job never knew about this conversation. He never knew that God was the first one to speak or that in the midst of all of his personal battles, God was the controlling factor.

When God asked if he had considered His servant Job, Satan said, *"Does Job fear God for nought? Hast thou not put a hedge about him and his house and all that he has, on every side? Thou hast blessed the work of his hands, and his possessions have increased in the land. But put forth thy hand now, and touch all that he has, and he will curse thee to thy face"* (1:9b–11). Satan was sneering to God about man, saying that man does not mean what he says in his worship of God.

This is in contrast to the first time Satan appeared on the scene of human history. In Genesis 3 Satan said, *"Did God say, 'You shall not eat of any tree of the garden'?"* When the woman answered, quoting what God actually did say, Satan replied, *"You will not die. For God knows that when you eat of it your eyes will be opened, and you will be like God, knowing good and evil"* (Gen. 3:1–5). In this case, Satan was sneering to man about God, claiming that God does not mean what He says. Then in the prelude to the Book of Job he turned to God and sneered about man, claiming that all man may say to God in worship is really meaningless. If man suffers, he will turn away from God.

When the scene in heaven was complete, Satan began to carry out the work which God had given him permission to do. Chapter 1:13–19 describes the awesome sequence where Job was informed of the loss of his oxen, his asses, his sheep, his servants, his camels, and finally even his own sons and daughters. Then Job came out with that great statement of faith in God. *"Naked I came from my mother's womb, and naked shall I return; the Lord gave, and the Lord has taken away; blessed be the name of the Lord"* (1:21).

The scene shifted back to heaven. Once again Satan came, and when God questioned him about Job, he responded with another sneer. *"Skin for skin! All that a man has he will give for his life. But put forth thy hand now, and touch his bone and his flesh, and he will curse thee to thy face"* (2:4b,5). So the battle continued. God, who will not tempt a man above what he is able to bear, gave Satan further permission. *"Behold, he is in your power; only spare his life"* (2:6b).

Satan went forth. Once more the scene reverted to the earth. Suddenly we find Job *"afflicted . . . with loathsome sores from the sole of his foot to the crown of his head. And he took a potsherd with which to scrape himself, and sat among the ashes"* (2:7b,8).

Notice here that Satan went every bit as far as God permitted him to go. When God told him that he could not touch Job, but that he could touch all that Job possessed, Satan did precisely that. He wiped out all of Job's material possessions. Then when God gave Satan permission to touch Job's body but not his life, Satan did precisely that. Job did not suffer from a headache or a stomach-ache, he suffered from the sole of his foot to the crown of his head. Each part of his body was touched as Satan went to the limits of his power.

Job still had no idea of what was transpiring. God and Satan were engaged in battle. The battleground was the body and soul of Job, and he had not been consulted!

So Job faced the dark night of unspeakable suffering with no explanation whatsoever.

Alexander Whyte, the Scottish preacher, states, ". . . till Christ came, no soul was ever made such a battleground between heaven and hell, as Job's soul was made."[2]

What were the issues raised in this time of suffering? First, Job and his friends found that, on the human level, life is not rational. Human reason was incapable of producing an explanation of what Job was suffering. Facing facts honestly led only to despair.

Some time ago my family and I traveled by train across the Isthmus of Panamá from Cristóbal to Balboa. Our eleven-

---

[2]Alexander Whyte, *Bible Characters.* Volume I, The Old Testament. Grand Rapids, Mich.: Zondervan Publishing House, 1952, p. 379.

year-old daughter, Beth, sitting next to me, became very pensive. She had seen some pathetic beggars in Cristóbal and began to ask me penetrating questions. She asked first why beggars do not work. I pointed out that in some cases beggars are unable to work. They may have physical handicaps which make it impossible. She by-passed that answer by saying that many beggars look as though they are capable of working. Therefore, why don't they? I said that in some economies there is not enough work for every man. We talked about a land like India where the economy cannot support all the people and consequently thousands die from starvation. It was not long before Beth was in tears. The answers I was giving did not satisfy the probing questions of her young mind. Finally she said, "Then what chance does a poor man have?"

Her questions went on a little further. Next she said, "If God is so great, why doesn't He do something about it?" My back was to the wall. How could I answer a question like that?

If all of life were rational, if all of life could be categorized and explained, if no tragedy remained at the back of human life, if there were no gap between God and man, then, as Oswald Chambers has said, the redemption of Jesus Christ is "much ado about nothing." The very fact that God became man and suffered the ignominious death on a Roman cross is evidence enough that life as we know it is *not* rational, and that there *is* a gap between God and man which only redemption can span.

A second issue, closely related to the first, is that some suffering cannot be explained. For Job and his friends, there was no possible way to explain the things they were facing. It was the frustration of trying to piece together a jigsaw puzzle when some of the pieces are missing.

In January, 1956, five young American missionaries were murdered by the Auca Indians in Ecuador. At the time this seemed like a senseless tragedy. But as months passed, the pieces of the puzzle began to fit together. Today it is easier to understand God's purpose in allowing that to happen, as some of those very killers have now come to know God.

One week after that tragedy, I was seated in the jungle home of my sister Elisabeth, the widow of Jim Elliot, one of the five victims. We were listening to news on the radio. Suddenly the word came that Lester Burton, of the Latin America Mission, who had been returning to Costa Rica by car from furlough, had died unexpectedly at the border of Nicaragua and Costa Rica. While waiting for the customs officials to arrive, he had taken a quick swim in a nearby river. This happens to be the only area in the world where fresh-water sharks exist. Les had taken a few strokes from the bank of the river when he was suddenly struck by a shark. He managed to get back onto the beach, where he collapsed and died in a matter of moments from loss of blood—a sudden, tragic, and unexplainable death.

We had great plans for Les on his return from furlough. He was to head up the L.A.M.'s camping program as well as to carry out rural church work in the town of Santo Domingo. At the time, his death seemed senseless. Now, years later, we have no further light as to why God took him so suddenly. His wife, Helen, had been widowed for a second time as she watched him die on the beach. Who can explain such suffering?

First, it becomes evident in Job that there were certain things which Job could not see but which today, with the benefit of hindsight, we can understand. With the Apostle James we can say, *"Behold, we call those happy who were steadfast. You have heard of the steadfastness of Job, and you have seen the purpose of the Lord, how the Lord is compassionate and merciful"* (James 5:11). Job could not see the purpose of the Lord, but in looking back at the prologue and the epilogue to the Book of Job, we can see God's purposes.

A second thing which Job had no way of knowing was that hundreds of years later, in a garden outside Jerusalem, a stone would roll away from a tomb and the Son of God, who had been dead, would walk forth alive. Suffering and sin, death and the devil, were conquered at that moment. But Job did not know this as he faced his own suffering.

With the benefit of hindsight, we can also see that God does not always explain Himself. He never once made His way clear to Job.

> *For my thoughts are not your thoughts,*
> *neither are your ways my ways, says the Lord.*
> *For as the heavens are higher than the earth,*
> *so are my ways higher than your ways*
> *and my thoughts than your thoughts* (Isa. 55:8,9).

Even when God spoke at the end, He did not answer the questions which Job raised. All He does is to raise further questions. But in so doing He meets the need of Job's heart for a personal encounter with God.

Job did not need all of his questions answered when he met God and heard Him speak. Answers became irrelevant. The real issue was his relationship to God.

> *God moves in a mysterious way,*
> *His wonders to perform;*
> *He plants His footsteps in the sea,*
> *And rides upon the storm.*
>
> *Deep in unfathomable mines*
> *Of never-failing skill*
> *He treasures up His bright designs,*
> *And works His sovereign will.*
>
> *Ye fearful saints, fresh courage take;*
> *The clouds ye so much dread*

Are big with mercy, and shall break
In blessings on your head.

Judge not the Lord by feeble sense,
But trust Him for His grace;
Behind a frowning providence
He hides a smiling face.

His purposes will ripen fast,
Unfolding every hour;
The bud may have a bitter taste,
But sweet will be the flower.

Blind unbelief is sure to err,
And scan His work in vain;
God is His own interpreter,
And He will make it plain.
                              William Cowper

III

"Oh, That I Knew Where I Might Find Him!"
(Job, ch.3 et al.)

What was Job actually facing? We cannot understand human life and God's ways with men by simply studying the ordinary run of life. We must also face the extraordinary and the tragic.

Those who delve deep into the issues of life—men like Job and David and Paul, who struggled with the fundamental issues of life—can help us to understand what life is about and what our relationship to God should be.

I once talked with a leader of a certain Christian organization concerning the methods that his group used in witnessing. He seemed to believe that he had all the answers and that the answers were always the same, no matter what the particular problems were.

Not long before that I had spoken on the campus of the Massachusetts Institute of Technology in a dormitory discussion. Here I found myself on the griddle. The students were raising burning questions. They wanted to know what the Bible says about Vietnam. Is the Gospel relevant to the racial issue? What does the Bible say about poverty? They were talking about real issues, but the answers were not easy. So I asked this particular man, "What do you say when people ask, 'What relevance does the Gospel have for Vietnam? What relevance does it have to the civil rights issue?'"

"Those aren't problems," he said. "We don't even discuss that. Those are just red herrings to get you away from the real point."

These *are* real issues that people live and struggle with. Try to tell the people of Vietnam that war is just a red herring to get them away from the real issues! These things have to be faced, and it is men like Job who help us to face them.

Can a man really know God? What is his relationship to God? What are God's ways with man? These are the questions that Job struggles with.

Job is faced with a number of great problems. The first one is physical suffering. This is what started the whole thing.

We have already noted that Satan was limited in his power. God told him just how far he could go, Satan went to these limits, and Job suffered the consequences. This happened so fast that Job hardly understood what had taken place. Here he was, wiped out economically, in the worst kind of physical suffering, sitting in ashes scratching himself and wondering what to do.

One sad element becomes evident at this point. There is no indication that anyone did anything to alleviate Job's physical suffering. His wife had some answers for him, but no physical alleviation. To her it was a simple matter: "Curse God and die, Job. Get it over with." Job's friends came along with philosophical and theological arguments. They could tell Job how it all started and the reasons behind it. But no one had any interest in helping him physically.

One of the bitterest memories I have of my own attempts to minister to people goes back to college days. On Saturday nights a group of us used to go into Chicago to witness to the men on Skid Row. One winter night I was talking with a shivering man slumped against a street lamp about the needs of his soul. A cold wind was blowing. Finally he turned to me and in the most pathetic way said, "Hey look, friend, would you buy me a bowl of soup?" I had been warned not to give anything to these alcoholics. They would spend it on liquor. It did not occur to me that he was not asking for money. He was not asking for liquor. He wanted a bowl of warm soup in his stomach. He was cold and hungry.

I said, "No! I've got something better to give you. I'm giving you Jesus Christ." He turned away with a disappointed look on his face and stood staring into the gutter while I talked about his soul. Finally he turned back a second time and said, "Hey look, buddy, won't you buy me a bowl of soup?" And I said, "No! I'm trying to give you something better."

How I wish I could live that day over! I would buy him ten bowls of soup! Here was a man in desperate physical need and I had no interest. How could I get through to his soul when he was standing there shivering, cold and hungry? I was talking about matters that held no interest for him at that moment. He wanted something warm in his stomach. That was the issue for him and I was not willing to face it. It would have cost only fifteen cents to buy him a bowl of soup and I could have done that. But I didn't.

Job's second problem was intellectual. His friends had a creed based on logic. They had an easy explanation for things. But Job was faced with a wildness in his own experience, a tragedy beyond comprehension. Easy explanations simply would not suffice. Job was revolting against easy answers. The man who has faced bereavement and suffering which does not fit the usual mold of platitudinous answers will empathize with Job. Explanations of why things have gone wrong do not delve deeply enough to meet the need of the human heart in the midst of unspeakable suffering. There is a perverseness in life that cannot be explained away by platitudes.

This is what Job struggled with. There were problems to be faced, and the easy answers that his friends were trying to give him did not satisfy his intellectual longings.

Did you ever notice how many times Job asked the question, "Why?"

In Chapter 3 he asked why he was ever born.

> *Why did I not die at birth,*
> *come forth from the womb and expire?*
> *Why did the knees receive me?*
> *Or why the breasts, that I should suck?* (3:11,12).

> *Or why was I not as a hidden untimely birth,*
> *as infants that never see the light?* (3:16).

"It would have been better if I hadn't been born. Or if I was born, why didn't I die at birth?"

> *Why is light given to him that is in misery,*
> *and life to the bitter in soul . . .?* (3:20).

"I'd rather die, but life is given to me."

> *Why is light given to a man whose way is hid,*
> *whom God has hedged in?* (3:23).

"I am hedged in by God. Why does He keep me alive?"

> *If I sin, what do I do to thee, thou watcher of men?*
> *Why hast thou made me thy mark?*
> *Why have I become a burden to thee?*
> *Why dost thou not pardon my transgression*
> *and take away my iniquity?* (7:20,21).

> *I shall be condemned;*
> *why then do I labor in vain?* (9:29).

"What's the use of all this? I'm going to be condemned in the end anyway." At this point Job was really pessimistic.

HOW COME, GOD?

Why dost thou hide thy face,
and count me as thy enemy? (13:24).

"Why should God treat me this way? I can't understand."

As for me, is my complaint against man?
Why should I not be impatient? (21:4).

Here he was asking a question that had some real basis to it.
"Why shouldn't I be impatient?"

Why do the wicked live,
reach old age, and grow mighty in power? (21:7).

In the rest of this chapter he was asking the same question,
"What about the wicked? They live a long time. They have all
kinds of power, riches, and wealth. Why do the wicked have
this, and why should I be suffering this way?"

Why are not times of judgment kept by the Almighty,
and why do those who know him never see his days? (24:1).

"Why doesn't God make more of Himself known to us?"
Look at some of the other problems he raised.

One dies in full prosperity,
being wholly at ease and secure,
his body full of fat
and the marrow of his bones moist.
Another dies in bitterness of soul,
never having tasted of good (21:23–25).

Why is it that some people in the world can live all their
days full of ease and security, and someone else dies in
bitterness of soul, never having tasted of good? I see the little
street urchins in Bogotá, Colombia. They were born in
corruption and poverty. They were turned out into the streets
when they could barely walk. All their lives they run up and
down those streets in poverty. And they die in bitterness of

soul, never having had a chance to taste of anything good. These were true facts that Job was dealing with.

And then,

> *They lie down alike in the dust,*
> *and the worms cover them* (21:26).

They are both at the same place at the end. Both the rich man who lived in fatness and the poor man who never tasted of good, in the end lie down in the same grave and worms cover them. Job cannot fathom this.

Job even sounds as though he were speaking of Vietnam:

> *From out of the city the dying groan,*
> *and the soul of the wounded cries for help;*
> *yet God pays no attention to their prayer* (24:12).

That was surely the way it looked to Job. And it must have looked that way to a lot of people in Vietnam. Many Christians there must have cried out in agony, "Is God paying no attention to my prayer?"

Job's third problem was emotional strain. His friends came and sat with him, but what kind of friends did they become? At one point Job finally cried out, *"Miserable comforters are you all"* (16:2). "You come here to comfort me, but instead you accuse me."

There should have been one person he could turn to. At least he should have been able to go home at night and pour out his heart to his wife. But when he turned to her, she said, "Job, curse God, and die! Get it over with!" He found no comfort from the one who was closest to him and who ought to have been the greatest help.

But Job responded, *"You speak as one of the foolish women would speak. Shall we receive good at the hand of God, and shall we not receive evil?"* (2:10). Job was much more realistic than she was.

HOW COME, GOD?

Happy is the man who can turn to a sympathetic wife. Job could not, and the emotional strain that must have built up when his wife failed him is beyond comprehension.

Then the rest of his family and household turned against him. In Chapter 19 Job found himself in a position of terrible loneliness.

> *He has put my brethren far from me,*
> * and my acquaintances are wholly estranged from me.*
> *My kinsfolk and my close friends have failed me;*
> * the guests in my house have forgotten me;*
> *my maidservants count me as a stranger;*
> * I have become an alien in their eyes.*
> *I call to my servant, but he gives me no answer;*
> * I must beseech him with my mouth.*
> *I am repulsive to my wife,*
> * loathsome to the sons of my own mother.*
> *Even young children despise me;*
> * when I rise they talk against me.*
> *All my intimate friends abhor me,*
> * and those whom I loved have turned against me* (19:13–19).

I remember a man who had been a priest in Bolivia for eighteen years. Then through the study of Scripture he came into a personal relationship with Jesus Christ. He left Bolivia and attended seminary in Costa Rica to get oriented in biblical studies. He once said to me, "Did you ever stop to think whom a priest can love? It's natural to love, and there must be an object of your love. You have a wife and children. You can pour out your love to them. Whom can a priest love? The only outlet I ever had was my mother. All of my natural love that ordinarily would go to a wife or to children went to my mother."

Then he said, "When I left the priesthood my own mother, the one I loved, said, 'Adrián, you are no longer my son. Don't ever come home again.'"

"Those whom I loved have turned against me." This, to Adrián, was one of the deepest issues that he had to face. The theological and the intellectual problems were great, but they did not compare to the emotional issues. He said, "You will never understand this. You can't conceive what this means to me."

This is what Job was enduring. There was hopelessness involved in this. If he had had any kind of hope, it might have been easier. But Job again and again lost his hope.

Occasionally there is a little glimmer of hope that comes out in the Book of Job. Unfortunately, the most frequently quoted verses from Job are those representing the attitude that he least exhibited. We quote the verse, *"I know that my Redeemer lives"* (19:25). That is said only once in the Book of Job. There are many other verses where he speaks about his hopelessness and his sense of lostness. It is only once in a while that we catch this glimmer of light.

Notice how he talks about hope in Chapter 14. Even the things of nature have hope:

> *For there is hope for a tree,*
> *   if it be cut down, that it will sprout again,*
> *   and that its shoots will not cease.*
> *Though its roots grow old in the earth,*
> *   and its stump die in the ground,*
> *yet at the scent of water it will bud*
> *   and put forth branches like a young plant.*
> *But man dies, and is laid low;*
> *   man breathes his last, and where is he?* (14:7–10).

Here is a cry of hopelessness. He said, "I don't have as much hope as a tree has." A tree can fall and can sprout again. Man goes down to earth and is put in the grave.

This led to the fourth great problem: the spiritual darkness which engulfed him. Physical suffering was bad enough but nothing like the intellectual confusion. And that was not as bad as the emotional strain. But the spiritual darkness that this produced was by far the worst.

In Chapter 3 he talked about being hemmed in.

> *Why is light given to a man whose way is hid,*
> *whom God has hedged in?* (3:23).

> *I am not at ease, nor am I quiet;*
> *I have no rest; but trouble comes* (3:26).

Again in Chapter 19:

> *Know then that God has put me in the wrong,*
> *and closed his net about me.*
> *Behold, I cry out, "Violence!" but I am not answered;*
> *I call aloud, but there is no justice.*
> *He has walled up my way, so that I cannot pass,*
> *and he has set darkness upon my paths.*
> *He has stripped from me my glory,*
> *and taken the crown from my head.*
> *He breaks me down on every side, and I am gone,*
> *and my hope has he pulled up like a tree* (19:6–10).

Here is the cry of a man in spiritual darkness.

Then comes that desperate cry in Chapter 23: *"Oh, that I knew where I might find him . . . !"* (23:3a). He was in darkness, and he could not find God.

He had not lost his faith in God. Job held on to that all the way through. But he honestly admitted from the depths of his soul that he had no idea where God was. Job was in blackness.

> *I would lay my case before him*
> *and fill my mouth with arguments.*
> *I would learn what he would answer me*
> *Would he contend with me . . . ?*
> *No; he would give heed to me"* (23:4–6).

"I believe God would actually listen to me if I could only find Him. The problem is that I cannot find Him."

"Oh, That I Knew Where I Might Find Him"

Behold, I go forward, but he is not there;
and backward, but I cannot perceive him;
on the left hand I seek him, but I cannot behold him;
I turn to the right hand, but I cannot see him (23:8,9).

In verse 10 we find one of the great keys to the Book of Job.
"I cannot find God. I go forward, backward, left, right; he is
not there. . . . *But he knows the way that I take.*"

"I do not know where He is, but thank God, He knows
where I am. I do not know what God is doing. But I know one
thing: God has not lost sight of me. He knows exactly where I
am: *he knows the way that I take; when he has tried me, I shall come
forth as gold*" (23:10). Here is the note of triumph, a glimpse of
light. God had not lost control.

Earlier we noticed that it was God who started the whole
thing in the council chambers of heaven. He was the first one
who spoke, not Satan. Having started it all, God knew exactly
what was going on. Job could not understand it. He never
knew what happened there in heaven. But in all of his darkness
he cried out, "I don't know where He is, but I know enough
about God to believe that He knows where I am."

The New Testament helps us to understand this. In the
New Testament we see things that Job never saw. Somewhere
in the Old Testament history, God had to make clear to His
people that He could work out His purposes through suffering, because this was what He was going to do at the cross. His
perfect plan of redemption would be fulfilled through suffering. Somehow God's people had to be prepared for this. So we
have the Book of Job.

We see a man groping in darkness. But he is a man still held
by God. We have to go to the cross to find the explanation.

Dr. Edmund Clowney of Westminster Theological Seminary, in a paper on "The Sovereignty of God and the Lostness of Man," says:

HOW COME, GOD?

We learn of the depth of human lostness and the height of divine holiness at the cross of Christ. Gather all your doubts about the reality of man's evil and the justice of God's wrath and come to the cross. But be prepared to stay. Stay till you sense something of the love of the Father for His only begotten and Beloved Son. Stay till the cry of the abandoned Sufferer breaks out of the scabbard of familiarity and pierces your heart. "Eloi, Eloi, Lama Sabachthani?" "Why?" he cries. "Why, my God, hast thou forsaken me?" He prayed that the cup might pass from Him. Now He drinks it. He is accursed and forsaken. The soldiers hear and mock.

The Father hears. What is His answer? That was the hour in history when it appeared that God was dead. The promises of the covenant seemed to fail for the One who had fulfilled all righteousness. Who can enter here? We cannot taste the cup Christ drank, but we know that He had to drink it.

Were perishing not what it must be, there could have been another answer to Christ's "Why?" But there is no other answer.[3]

When you and I can answer the question "Why?" that Christ asked on the cross, then perhaps we can answer some of these other questions. But there is no answer given, except this, that God in His own way was working out His perfect plan.

And Job says, "I don't know where He is. I cannot find Him. *But he knows the way that I take; when he has tried me, I shall come forth as gold*" (23:10).

[3]Edmund Clowney, "The Sovereignty of God and the Lostness of Man." *Evangelical Missions Quarterly*, Vol. 4, No. 4 (Summer, 1968), pp. 224–225.

IV

"Who That Was Innocent Ever Perished?"
(Eliphaz, chs. 4, 5)

Job's three friends now begin to deal with his problems and to offer their solutions. The first spokesman is Eliphaz. Let's look at his declarations.

First, Eliphaz's basic problem was to reconcile his own beliefs with what had happened to Job. Eliphaz had his creed, as did the other men. Their creeds were similar, as was Job's before this happened to him. Each of them had a fairly good idea of how God should work under certain circumstances. But Job's situation did not fit. They were faced with the dual problem of holding on to their beliefs and of explaining what had happened to Job.

They were hit desperately by Job's calamities. They really believed that Job had been a good man. But why, then, should he suffer so? With great agony of soul they must have come to the conclusion that their own beliefs had to be right and therefore Job had to be wrong. Once this conclusion was reached, an inevitable "holier than thou" attitude developed.

Their creed said that God had to work in a given way under certain circumstances. Job did not fit into this, so the problem must lie with Job and not with their creed. All of Job's experience—his struggle to relate to God, his struggle with suffering—had to take second place in order that their theology would not be shaken. He—not their theology—must be wrong.

Eliphaz would have done better to keep quiet. There are times in the face of suffering when silence is the best we can offer a friend.

When Job's friends first came, they did keep quiet. Probably those first seven days were the best, as far as Job was concerned, in his relationship with those men. They knew he was suffering, and he knew that they had come to comfort him. They did not have to say anything. Once they started to talk, they ruined whatever help they had given. The remainder of the book is one long argument.

When my grandfather was dying, my father spent much time at his bedside. My father spoke afterward of how our pastor would visit during the final days. "Mr. McCoy would come into the living room and just sit down. He did not ask to go into the sickroom. He did not even come to talk to me. He just wanted me to know that in this difficult time he was here. If he could be of any help, that was what he wanted. But he would seldom say a word."

Joseph Bayly, who has three sons in heaven and thus knows more about grief than most of us, writes:

> We are most likely to be helpful with an economy of words. In our contacts with people at death as at other times, it is easy to say too much, to talk when we ought to listen.
>
> Sensitivity in the presence of grief should usually make us more silent, more listening.
>
> I was sitting, torn by grief. Someone came and talked to me of God's dealing, of why it happened, of hope beyond the grave. He talked constantly, he said things I knew were true.
>
> I was unmoved, except to wish he'd go away. He finally did.

Another came and sat beside me. He didn't talk. He didn't ask leading questions. He just sat beside me for an hour and more, listened when I said something, answered briefly, prayed simply, left.

I was moved. I was comforted. I hated to see him go.[4]

It is very easy to argue as Eliphaz was doing, on the basis of precedent, because it gives a simple answer. To argue that way is risky, however, because God does not necessarily follow precedents. He does not say that because He did a certain thing at a given point in history, He will do it the same way now.

We like to quote verses such as *"Jesus Christ is the same yesterday, and today and for ever"* (Heb. 13:8). *"I the Lord do not change"* (Mal. 3:6). Those verses are as true as any other verses in the Bible, but stop to think what the verse says. *"I the Lord do not change."* He does not say, "I do not change my ways of dealing with you." God never says that, because He does change His ways of dealing with us. The way God dealt with Abraham was not the way He dealt with Moses. What He did with Peter was not what He did with Paul. Here Eliphaz had a basic error in his thinking. "God has dealt this way with me and everyone else I have known, so He has to deal this way with Job." Here his argument broke down. God was not going to be bound in that way.

This led him to his basic thesis—that suffering is the result of sin. Eliphaz's speeches are found in Chapters 4 and 5, Chapter 15, and Chapter 22.

In Chapter 4, he laid out his thesis:

> *Think now, who that was innocent ever perished?*
> *Or where were the upright cut off?*

[4]Joseph T. Bayly, *The View from a Hearse.* Elgin, Ill.: David C. Cook Publishing Co., 1969, pp. 40–41.

> *As I have seen, those who plow iniquity*
> *and sow trouble reap the same,*
> *By the breath of God they perish,*
> *and by the blast of his anger they are consumed* (4:7–9).

There was his simple argument: the man who rebels against God suffers the consequences and is consumed by the breath of God. There is truth here, of course. But it does not necessarily mean that he will suffer the consequences immediately.

This was what Satan said to Eve in the Garden of Eden, "The day that you eat thereof, God says that you will die, but you shall not surely die." Satan was right up to a point; she did not die physically the day she ate that fruit. As a matter of fact, Adam lived over nine hundred years. I do not know when he ate that fruit, but he probably lived hundreds of years afterward. But sin entered in and death by sin, so he died spiritually right away and physically later on.

However, Eliphaz claimed that the man who sinned would suffer immediately for his sin. Conversely, when a man suffered, it was because he had been a great sinner.

Notice Eliphaz's logic. Once the basic premise is accepted, his arguments are almost undebatable. He next said that man is inherently evil.

> *Can mortal man be righteous before God?*
> *Can a man be pure before his Maker?* (4:17).

No argument there. What man could claim to be pure before his Maker? Impossible! The closer one gets to his Maker, the more he recognizes his own impurity. Eliphaz was right.

> *Even in his servants he puts no trust,*
> *and his angels he charges with error;*
> *how much more those who dwell in houses of clay,*
> *whose foundation is in the dust,*
> *who are crushed before the moth* (4:18,19).

We have no argument. Man basically is a sinner.

He has already said that suffering is the result of sin. Now every man is a sinner. Therefore, the logical conclusion is that every man has to suffer. Suffering becomes an inherent part of man.

> *For affliction does not come from the dust,*
> *nor does trouble sprout from the ground* (5:6).

These troubles do not come from outside. Where do they come from?

> *. . . man is born to trouble*
> *as the sparks fly upward* (5:7).

He is born in sin. He is born to trouble.

Hebrew scholars have pointed out that by simply changing certain vowel points in verse 7, this could be translated: "It is man who begets trouble, as the sparks fly upward." Trouble comes from man himself.

In verse 8, a bit of pride comes out:

> *As for me, I would seek God,*
> *and to God would I commit my cause* (5:8).

He was implying that Job had not sought God. "You are continuing to live in your suffering because you have not turned to God. If I were in your state, Job, I would seek God. I would commit my cause to God, *who does great things and unsearchable, marvelous things without number: he gives rain upon the earth and sends waters upon the fields"* (5:9,10).

Once again, there is a logic here—if a man does turn to God, he can find deliverance. But somehow Job's case still did not fit. This must have sounded like irony to Job when Eliphaz continued, *"Behold, happy is the man whom God reproves"* (5:17). Job did not know the source of his trouble, he certainly was not happy.

HOW COME, GOD?

> *. . . happy is the man whom God reproves;*
> *therefore despise not the chastening of the Almighty* (5:17).

"Don't despise it, Job. Accept it. Be happy about it." That is a miserable thing to tell a man who is sitting in ashes scraping himself and struggling with countless problems!

> *For he wounds, but he binds up;*
> *he smites, but his hands heal.*
> *He will deliver you from six troubles;*
> *in seven there shall no evil touch you* (5:18,19).

Yet what had happened just before this? Job had lost everything he had. Now to say that God would deliver him in six troubles, and in seven no evil would touch him, must have sounded like hollow mockery.

> *In famine he will redeem you from death,*
> *and in war from the power of the sword.*
> *You shall be hid from the scourge of the tongue,*

—he was not hid from the scourge of his friends' tongues—

> *and shall not fear destruction when it comes.*

—destruction had already come and destroyed everything that he had—

> *At destruction and famine you shall laugh,*

—Job was not laughing; he had nothing to laugh about. Yet Eliphaz was telling him, "Just laugh about it, Job. Destruction comes, and you'll laugh at it. It is not really going to hurt you"—

> [You] *shall not fear the beasts of the earth.*
> *For you shall be in league with the stones of the field,*
> *and the beasts of the field shall be at peace with you.*
> *You shall know that your tent is safe,*

—his tent was not safe; his house had been destroyed—

> *and you shall inspect your fold and miss nothing.*

46

—he had just lost all the cattle that he had; he did not have a
horse left in the barn—

> *You shall know also that your descendants shall be many,*
> *and your offspring as the grass of the earth* (5:20–25).

That is a great way to talk to a man who has lost ten children.
What kind of offspring did Job have to talk about?

Then Eliphaz came to his final conclusion.

> *Lo, this we have searched out; it is true.*
> *Hear, and know it for your good* (5:27).

"Job, just listen to what I have to say and know it for your own
good. I have searched this out and I know that it is true." Here
was a dogmatic man, and nothing that he said was of any use to
Job. It simply did not fit Job's case.

Up to this point, he had been arguing on the basis of his own
limited experience. But his experience did not include Job's
experience. Here Eliphaz's position breaks down.

V

"Have You Listened in the Council of God?"
(Eliphaz, chs. 15, 22)

Eliphaz's second speech is in Chapter 15. Each of the friends had now spoken and Job had answered. Eliphaz's turn came around again. He starts off by accusing Job of what he himself was guilty of.

> But you are doing away with the fear of God,
> and hindering meditation before God (15:4).

Eliphaz and his friends were the ones who were hindering meditation by arguing with Job and not giving him a chance to meditate. Yet he said, "Job, you are hindering meditation."

Then he began to tell Job that his experience was not what it ought to be. Eliphaz's experience did not include what Job had been through but he did not take this into account. He simply went on as though he knew everything that Job knew.

Huxley, the great agnostic, is reputed to have said that he objected to Christians because they knew too much about God. Perhaps he had some basis for his objection. Sometimes we get very dogmatic about who God is and how He will work. We know so much about God that we do not allow the other fellow to fit into the picture.

Eliphaz's logic continued unimpeachable, if we accept his basic premise. One can prove anything by logic. Mark Twain, you may remember, proved by logic that he was his own grandfather. But it is dangerous to assume that one's conclusions are correct, if the premise is wrong.

Some years ago in Colombia I received a letter of resignation from two of our finest national workers. It was written in very bitter terms against the Latin America Mission and the missionaries. A few days later I received a similar letter of resignation from one of our missionaries. The situation was so serious that Kenneth Strachan, general director of the mission, came to Colombia to help me deal with it. During his visit, one of those who had resigned made this statement to him: "When I see a missionary do such and such, what can I conclude except that the missionary is insincere and dishonest? I can't conclude anything else."

But Ken answered, "Wait a minute. Yes, you can conclude something else. You can conclude that perhaps you don't have all the facts."

I learned a real lesson there. It looked very unimpeachable to argue a certain way, saying, "This and this I see; therefore, this is the only possible conclusion." Ken said, "No. Maybe you don't have all the facts."

Here was Eliphaz's problem. He did not have all the facts—and neither did Job. They never saw what went on in heaven between God and Satan. They were never allowed into those council chambers of God. They were debating on a human plane, without having all the facts.

Eliphaz not only argued from his own experience, but he refused to accept Job's experience as valid. He had to pour Job into his mold. He argued as though he knew everything Job knew.

> *Are you the first man that was born?*
> *Or were you brought forth before the hills?*
> *Have you listened in the council of God?* (15:7,8a).

No, Job hadn't, and neither had Eliphaz. They did not hear that conversation between Satan and God. But Eliphaz acted as though he had.

> *And do you limit wisdom to yourself?*
> *What do you know that we do not know?* (15:8b,9a).

The obvious answer is that Job knew a lot they did not know. What did Eliphaz know about losing ten children? What did Eliphaz know about having his house and lands destroyed? What did Eliphaz know about losing his health and being covered with boils from the top of his head to the bottom of his feet? Yet he dared to say to Job, *"What do you know that we do not know? What do you understand that is not clear to us?"*

Eliphaz . . . tries to wear down Job's opposition by sheer ponderosity; i.e., saying *nothing* with terrific emphasis. Then, like a theological buzzard, he sits on the perch of massive tradition and preens his ruffled feathers and croaks his eloquent platitudes."[5]

This attitude—that everything has to fit into his experience—led Eliphaz to another step, his worst yet. His last speech is in Chapter 22. Here we find him stooping very low, because he still had not been able to fit Job into his little creed. So he made up stories about Job:

> *Is not your wickedness great?*
> *There is no end to your iniquities.*

---

[5]Oswald Chambers, *Baffled to Fight Better*. London: Oswald Chambers Publications Association and Marshall, Morgan & Scott, 1931, p. 53.

> For you have exacted pledges of your brothers for nothing,
>   and stripped the naked of their clothing.
> You have given no water to the weary to drink,
>   and you have withheld bread from the hungry.
> The man with power possessed the land,
>   and the favored man dwelt in it.
> You have sent widows away empty,
>   and the arms of the fatherless were crushed.
> Therefore snares are round about you,
>   and sudden terror overwhelms you;
> your light is darkened, so that you cannot see,
>   and a flood of water covers you (22:5–11).

Compare that with God's words, when He said to Satan, *"Have you considered my servant Job, that there is none like him on the earth, a blameless and upright man, who fears God and turns away from evil?"* (1:8). When we read what God and then Eliphaz said about Job, I think we do have all the facts and can come to only one conclusion: Eliphaz was lying. God would not have called Job a *"blameless"* man if he had *"given no water to the weary to drink,"* or *"withheld bread from the hungry,"* if he had turned away the widows *"empty, and the arms of the fatherless were crushed."* Eliphaz was fabricating lies about Job so that he would not have to lose his creed.

Then he went further. He spoke some erroneous ideas about God.

> Is it any pleasure to the Almighty if you are righteous,
>   or is it gain to him if you make your ways blameless? (22:3).

He is saying, "What difference does it make to God whether you are righteous or sinful? It is no gain to God either way."

Of course it is. The whole thrust of the New Testament speaks about the holiness God wants in the heart of men. It certainly is a pleasure to God when a man is righteous. Yet Eliphaz, in order to hold his own viewpoint, was talking as though God didn't really care about what went on among men.

51

Here is the heart of the problem. Does God have an interest in man? Can man know God? Is there any relationship man can have with God?

Eliphaz went one step further. He talks in irrelevant terms to Job. He did that earlier, but it was far worse by the end of this speech.

> *Agree with God, and be at peace;*
> *thereby good will come to you* (22:21).

Once again Eliphaz says what from one angle is perfectly true. Think, for instance, of a man alienated from God by sin, who has never come into a relationship with Jesus Christ. When God convicts him of sin, we can say, "Agree with God that you are a sinner. Accept what God gives you in Jesus Christ; and then come into peace with God."

But this did not fit Job. Job said, "I want to agree with God, but I don't know what to agree with." When Eliphaz finished his speech, Job said, *"Oh, that I knew where I might find him"* (23:3a). I can't agree with God, because I don't know what He is trying to say to me. It isn't a question of finding out what God is saying to me. I don't know where He is."

It is easy to pass off platitudes to others in trouble, telling them, "Just agree with God; surrender to God; and the whole thing will come out all right." This may be completely irrelevant to the problem.

Several years ago in Cartagena, Colombia, a young American couple lost a two-year-old child in a sudden and unexplainable death. Not having lived long in Colombia, they wished to bury the child in the United States. Because of the law that burial must be within twenty-four hours, they had to leave immediately. I tried to help the husband get ready to leave; the poor wife was utterly crushed. Another missionary came and tried to encourage the young man. "Well, let me tell you, just trust the Lord. Just rest in His strong arms, and that's all you have to do." Then he turned and walked out.

What did that mean to a man who did not know God? He was trying to make arrangements to get the body of his child, his wife, and himself out of the country, and someone was telling him, "Just rest in His strong arms and it will be all right." It meant nothing to him.

This is what Eliphaz was doing. Then he brought up another point that was almost humorous:

If you return to the Almighty and humble yourself,
* if you remove unrighteousness far from your tents,*
if you lay gold in the dust,
* and gold of Ophir among the stones of the torrent bed,*
and if the Almighty is your gold,
* and your precious silver;*
then you will delight yourself in the Almighty (22:23–26a).

He was saying, "Job, if you will forget about gold—just lay all your money in the dust, and make God your gold, then in the Almighty you will delight yourself *and lift up your face to God.*"

What an irrelevant suggestion! The least problem Job was having at this point was the problem of money. It never came up once. This shows how far Eliphaz had gone.

Job responded with a tremendous outburst. His next two speeches are very long. Bildad barely got in another word and Zophar was left out on the final round. These men lost him completely. They had been dealing on a level where Job was simply not to be found, and thus did not communicate with him at all.

Experience was Eliphaz's standard for God. But experience is always inadequate by itself. The only real standard is what God has revealed in His word and in the person of Jesus Christ.

HOW COME, GOD?

What did He reveal about God? When He cried out in darkness and agony, *"Eloi, Eloi, lama sabach-thani?" "My God, my God, why hast thou forsaken me?"* (Mark 15:34), Christ was revealing that God could work out His purposes through suffering.

When Kenneth Strachan lay dying of cancer, his suffering was indescribable. His biographer writes:

> The days which followed were days of horror for Ken and for all who had to watch. . . . Latin Americans, North Americans, Christians and people who would hardly have known enough to call themselves Christians, prayed in every way they knew. There were those who prefaced every prayer with "If it be Thy will, Lord," and there were those who were sure enough of His will to see no need for such a preface. Some came to his hospital room to pray, and some tense little battles were waged across his bed between those who felt that no Christian has an inalienable right to claim physical healing, and those who believed that such an admission was a mere failure of faith, or worse still, an actual capitulation to Satan himself who held the sufferer in his grasp. There were those who wished to anoint Ken with oil . . . and those who asked to lay hands on him in prayer. He did not object to any of these gestures, although they sometimes made him feel surrounded by conflict and confusion.

(This is the way poor Job must have felt. His friends were arguing about the answers to his situation and all it did was surround him with conflict and confusion.)

> If his illness was in reality a diabolical attack he knew that he had better do some fervent praying and some strong resisting. If, on the other hand, it was a griddle on which God Himself had placed him in order to perfect in him the image of His Son, then his only obligation was to submit in trust and patience.
> "Who am I, that I can yak and expect God to come and rescue me out of this situation?" was the way he felt when he

talked to his sister. "We are not a privileged people, exempt from suffering."[6]

Ken believed in the sovereignty of God and knew that his own perspective was distorted.

This is something that Job's friends did not recognize. And although later Job realized it, even he did not know at one point that his own perspective was distorted.

Ken found the answer in the fact that God was a loving Father, no matter what the perspective might be. He knew that his own perspective was distorted, and "whatever my tiny contribution to God's pattern may be, He is a loving Father and looks upon me as His child."[7]

[6]Elisabeth Elliot, *Who Shall Ascend?* New York: Harper & Row, 1968, pp. 154, 155.
[7]*Ibid.*, p. 155.

VI

"Inquire ... of Bygone Ages"
(Bildad, chs. 8, 18, 25)

Bildad began with a repetition of the arguments that Eliphaz had presented. He maintained that the suffering of Job and of his family was a result of their sin.

> *If your children have sinned against him,*
> *he has delivered them into the power of their transgression* (8:4).

What a miserable way to comfort a person! Supposing he were right that Job's children had been destroyed because of their own sin? Is that the way to approach a man in need of comfort?

Once in Colombia I saw precisely this type of thing happen. Rafael Yepes was one of the original believers in the town of El Carmen de Bolívar. Dennis Crespo had let him to Christ, and Rafael became a pillar in the church. Then the church in El Carmen was shaken by the charismatic movement in its most extreme form. The pastor announced that he was going to preach on nothing but the Holy Spirit and the gifts of the Spirit until everyone in that church received the baptism of the Spirit.

Rafael Yepes was a more mature Christian than some of the

others, and he recognized the dangers of this. He was not against preaching on the Holy Spirit, but he was opposed to the extremes that accompanied it. Before long some wild manifestations began in the church, so extreme that the neighbors questioned what went on there. Rafael Yepes, who stood strongly against this and did his best to get them back to the Scriptures, was accused of resisting the Holy Spirit.

One night the pastor of the church organized a group of young people to go to his house and serenade him. They sang songs of invitation, such as *"Pecador, Ven a Cristo Jesus"* ("Sinner, Come to Christ Jesus"), as though he were not a Christian.

One morning, at 4:45, Rafael Yepes went out during a raging thunderstorm and was struck dead by either a bolt of lightning or a heart attack triggered by the lightning. When I went to El Carmen to participate in his funeral, I discovered that the pastor of the church and others had told Mrs. Yepes that he had committed the unpardonable sin of blaspheming against the Holy Spirit and this was his punishment! This they told her on the day of her husband's funeral!

It reminded me of Job's friends:

> *If your children have sinned against him,*
> *he has delivered them into the power of their transgression.*

Bildad next began to appeal to tradition:

> *For inquire, I pray you, of bygone ages,*
> *and consider what the fathers have found;*
> *for we are but of yesterday, and know nothing,*
> *for our days on earth are a shadow.*
> *Will they not teach you, and tell you,*
> *and utter words out of their understanding?* (8:8–10).

He was saying, "The fathers will tell us about this. Tradition will help us to understand. We are still young and do not understand these things; but these patriarchs can tell us. They have been through it."

Bildad was appealing to tradition instead of trying to formulate a theology adequate for the present crisis.

What had taken place in the past was not wrong. Nor were the views of the fathers necessarily wrong. They may have been perfectly right for their time. But it was useless for Bildad to say to Job, "You will find the answer to your problems in what the fathers have told us. These men have all been through it before and they know all about it." Many other people had suffered, but there had never been a case quite like this one. To say that the men of the past had the proper answer for the problem of the present was not sufficient.

It is easy to talk about "the good old days," referring to the past, and say, "Why can't we do the same thing today?" Why? The world changes. People change. Circumstances change. The answers of the past are not necessarily adequate for today. We must find God's answers for today.

One of the quickest ways to alienate today's student generation is to tell them that we do certain things because "this is the way it has always been done." Probably no previous generation has been so ready to break with the past and look to the present and the future. The problems of society today are screaming for solutions, and students do not believe that the solutions of the past are adequate for today. New answers must be found for the problems of a new age.

Even if it had been true that the patriarchs had suffered as Job, would that have made it any easier for Job? That would not have alleviated his suffering one bit. That would not have made those sores that he was constantly scratching stop itching, just because someone else had itched in the same way. That would not have made his emotional problems any less when his family and his friends turned against him. That would not have changed the horror of those intellectual problems that he struggled with. That would not have brought any light into the darkness of his spiritual isolation.

Tennyson caught this truth in his classic poem "In Memoriam." He spoke of those who say that suffering is the common lot of everyone. In the next verse he said:

> *That loss is common would not make*
> *My own less bitter, rather more:*
> *Too common! Never morning wore*
> *To evening, but some heart did break.*[8]

If every day someone's heart is broken, does that make it easier when my heart breaks?

Some time ago, I had to call a lady in Texas to tell her that her husband had died unexpectedly in Costa Rica that evening. Would it have been any easier if I had said to her, "Mrs. Rice, someone has died every minute around the world today. Lots of wives have lost their husbands today, so be comforted"? Would that have made her loss any less bitter?

Bildad's next speech, in Chapter 18, is a description of what happens to the wicked. However, the first part of the chapter gives a glimpse into something which Bildad himself did not fully understand. It is left to the Lord to develop this thought in Chapters 38 through 41. But Bildad struck on a truth when he said:

> *How long will you hunt for words? . .*
> *You who tear yourself in your anger,* `
> *   shall the earth be forsaken for you,*
> *   or the rock be removed out of its place?* (18:2,4).

He was saying, "Job, do you think that God is running the universe for your benefit? Do you think the whole world

[8]Alfred Tennyson, "In Memoriam," *The Poetical Works of Alfred Tennyson.* New York: Houghton Mifflin Co., n.d., p. 289.

revolves around you?" There is an element of truth there. He said to Job, "God is not going to interrupt the whole motion of the universe just for you."

Bildad did not fully understand this himself. It might have helped Job had he pursued this line. "Job, the world is not revolving around you. God has other plans besides you. You are part of the picture, but you are not the hub of the wheel." But, having barely said that much, he dropped it and went back to the old line of argument.

> *Yea, the light of the wicked is put out,*
> *and the flame of his fires does not shine.*
> *The light is dark in his tent,*
> *and his lamp above him is put out* (18:5,6).

The rest of Chapter 18 is a repetition of that theme.

Bildad's last contribution is in Chapter 25. This is the shortest speech of any of the friends. Yet here Bildad came closer to presenting some helpful thoughts than anywhere else in the book.

"Dominion and fear are with God" (25:2a). He recognized the great truth of the sovereignty of God. The Spanish version says, "Sovereignty is with God." All the dominion of the universe is in the hands of God. This is one of the keys to understanding the book.

"He makes peace in his high heaven" (25:2b). Not here on earth. Not on man's terms. But in heaven on His terms.

In warfare the conquering country spells out the peace terms, whether they are in the right or not. Of course, there has never been a war where all the right was on one side. But in man's relationship with God, it *is* this way. All the right is on God's side and all the wrong is on man's side. So God can spell out His peace terms in heaven. Man has to come to God's terms, not God to man's terms. We have nothing to commend

ourselves to Him, but He has everything to commend Himself
to us.

Then Bildad picked up the theme of man's vileness in the
sight of God.

> *How then can man be righteous before God?*
> *How can he who is born of woman be clean?*
> *Behold, even the moon is not bright*
> *and the stars are not clean in his sight;*
> *how much less man, who is a maggot,*
> *and the son of man, who is a worm!* (25:4–6).

There is real truth here. Yet, even at this point, he did not
come to grips with Job's problem. Job had already recognized
that man cannot commend himself to God. Who can be
righteous before God? Who can bring a clean thing out of an
unclean? So even though what Bildad said is true, it was not
particularly helpful to Job.

VII

"Less Than Your Guilt Deserves"
(Zophar, chs. 11, 20)

Now we turn to Zophar, who speaks in Chapter 11 and again in 20. In neither of these speeches did he produce anything particularly original, except that he was more vehement than the others in his denunciations of Job. Bildad was strong, but listen to Zophar:

> *Should a multitude of words go unanswered,*
> *and a man full of talk be vindicated?*
> *Should your babble silence men,*
> *and when you mock, shall not one shame you?*
> *For you say, "My doctrine is pure,*
> *and I am clean in God's eyes. . . .*
> *Know then that God exacts of you less than your guilt deserves*
> (11:2–4,6).

No one else had dared say this to Job.

Job had been contending that he was innocent, and that his sins did not merit this kind of punishment. Then Zophar speaks up, "Job, you have gotten off easily. God has given you less than your guilt deserves."

In the next verses he speaks a great truth, but again it was nothing new.

> *Can you find out the deep things of God?*
> *Can you find out the limit of the Almighty?*
> *It is higher than heaven—what can you do?*
> *Deeper than Sheol—what can you know?*
> *Its measure is longer than the earth,*
> *and broader than the sea.*
> *If he passes through, and imprisons,*
> *and calls to judgment, who can hinder him?* (11:7–10).

He was recognizing the sovereignty of God, but why say it? Job had just said the same thing in Chapter 9:10–12.

Zophar was no more helpful than Bildad. He was merely mouthing platitudes. Job had already seen the same truth.

The rest of Zophar's speech again talked about the wicked, except that he added several vituperations.

> *For he knows worthless men;*
> *when he sees iniquity, will he not consider it?*
> *But a stupid man will get understanding,*
> *when a wild ass's colt is born a man* (11:11–12).

The implication was, "Job, you are stupid. There is no more hope of your getting understanding than there is of a wild ass giving birth to a man."

In his second speech, in Chapter 20, Zophar did have one small contribution to make, but it was inadvertent. He revealed something about himself in the first thing that he said.

> *Then Zophar the Naamathite answered:*
> *Therefore my thoughts answer me,*
> *because of my haste within me* (20:1,2).

Here is a key to Zophar's problem. He was too hasty with what he had to say.

HOW COME, GOD?

> *I hear censure which insults me,*
> *and out of my understanding a spirit answers me* (20:3).

He could not wait to answer Job. And because of his haste he jumped to the wrong conclusions.

Haste can have devastating effects on theology and can result in a wrong view of God and man. Had Zophar taken time to reflect on what was transpiring between Job and God, he might have come to the correct conclusion that some sufferers are saints. Had he meditated long enough on the insights God provides elsewhere, he might even have seen that suffering and salvation are intertwined.

VIII

"The Outskirts of His Ways"
(Job, chs. 13, 26)

Now let's summarize briefly what these friends have said. Positively, two things can be said. First, they came to Job with right motives. Their friend was suffering, so they came to empathize with him. They sat in silence for seven days, which was the best thing they could have done. They might have done better had they continued to keep quiet, because they said nothing that helped Job very much. However, their motives were right. They did want to help.

Second, they grasped some aspects of truth. Not everything they said was false. Their problem was that they did not know how to apply the truth.

Negatively, five things can be noted.

First, there is no indication that the friends offered any physical help to Job. Nobody tried to salve his wounds.

Second, there is no indication that any of them ever prayed for or with Job. At the end, Job prayed for them. But as far as we know they never prayed for him.

Third, they rejected Job's sincerity. They did not accept his claims to innocence. They kept telling him, "Job, you know perfectly well that you are a sinner. These words cannot go unanswered. You know they are not true."

Interpersonal relationships break down when one cannot accept the sincerity of his brother in Christ. No matter how wrong we may think him to be, if we cannot accept his sincerity, we cut off any possibility of communication.

Several years ago in Colombia, one of our Colombian teachers decided to move to another city and work elsewhere. I wrote her a letter of gratitude expressing appreciation for her years of faithful service. We had had problems with her but I did not mention them in the letter of farewell, speaking honestly of her positive contributions.

She sent the letter back with a note saying, "I do not accept this letter because it is insincere."

I went to see her and asked, "Do you think that I wrote this letter in insincerity?"

"I surely do."

"Do you think that I told you deliberate lies?"

"Yes."

'Don't you think I could honestly express gratitude for the good contribution you have made without mentioning problems that have existed?"

"No, you are insincere."

And at that point all communication was broken off. This is what happened with Job's friends when they would not accept his sincerity.

Fourth, these friends rejected Job's experience as invalid. They had to protect their creed. But Job did not fit into it. He said, "My experience does not fit that way." "Well then, Job, your experience is wrong."

Finally, they defended their own views about God at the cost of love, understanding, compassion, and honesty. They even went to the extreme of telling lies about Job and about God. Job called them on this in Chapter 13.

As for you, you whitewash with lies;
worthless physicians are you all (13:4).

Will you speak falsely for God. . . ? (13:7a).

That word "for" is very important. He did not say, "Will you speak falsely about God?" These men were supposedly defending God. Instead, they were defending their view about God. They were saying things that were not true about God, in order that their creed would not crumble.

In *The Brothers Karamazov*, Dostoyevsky discusses what would have happened if Jesus Christ had come back to earth in the sixteenth century: He meets the "Grand Inquisitor," who tells Him that He is no longer needed. Now they have their own theology formulated. They know there are three things needed to build a strong church: miracle, mystery, authority. With miracles, you can deceive the people and make them do what you want. With mystery, you keep them with you out of curiosity. With authority, you keep them under control. The Grand Inquisitor points out to Jesus Christ that Satan gave Him a chance for all three of those things and He turned them down. He could have performed the miracle by turning the stones into bread but He refused. Mystery, yes; He could have jumped off the temple and not been destroyed. Authority; all the world could have been His, but He turned it down. Now it's too late. We've made our theology. Tomorrow we'll build the pyre and burn Him at the stake. He is no longer needed.

This is what Job's friends were doing. They had forgotten about God as a person. They were defending their theology at the cost of everything else. Controversy became the order of the day.

Alexander Whyte comments on this controversy:

> Like the Captain of Salvation Himself, Job, His forerunner, took up successful arms against a whole sea of sorrows, and he would have won every battle of them all had he only been able to bear up under the suspicious looks and the reproving speeches of his . . . friends. But what Satan could not do with all his Sabeans, and all his Chaldeans, and all his winds from the wilderness to help him, that he soon did with the help of the debating approaches and the controversial assaults of Eliphaz, and Zophar, and Bildad. . . . Oh, the unmitigable curse of controversy! Oh, the detestable passions that corrections and contradictions kindle up to a fury in the proud heart of man. Eschew controversy, my brethren, as you would eschew the entrance to hell itself. Let them have it their own way. Let them talk. Let them write. Let them correct you. Let them traduce you. Let them judge and condemn you. Let them slay you. Rather let the truth of God itself suffer, than that love suffer.[9]

Job's friends were not willing to let the truth of God, *as they understood it,* suffer. They would rather have love suffer. And so it did.

"You have not enough of the divine nature in you to be a controversialist," continues Whyte. "He was oppressed, and He was afflicted, yet He opened not His mouth. . . . Heal me, prays Augustine again and again, of this lust of mine of always vindicating myself."[10]

How did Job react to all of this? In Chapter 26 Job was still holding on to this great fact that he had propounded again and again: God is inscrutable in His ways and we cannot really understand what He is doing. Job never let go of his faith in God as sovereign.

---

[9]Alexander Whyte, *op. cit.*, pp. 379, 380.
[10]*Ibid.*, p. 380.

He stretches out the north over the void,
  and hangs the earth upon nothing.
He binds up the waters in his thick clouds,
  and the cloud is not rent under them.
He covers the face of the moon,
  and spreads over it his cloud.
He has described a circle upon the face of the waters
  at the boundary between light and darkness.
The pillars of heaven tremble,
  and are astounded at his rebuke.
By his power he stilled the sea;
  by his understanding he smote Rahab.
By his wind the heavens were made fair;
  his hand pierced the fleeing serpent.
Lo, these are but the outskirts of his ways (26:7–14a).

"All the things we have been talking about," Job said, "are barely the fringes of the ways of God. We still have not come to the heart of it. Maybe we never will."

And how small a whisper do we hear of him!
But the thunder of his power who can understand? (26:14b).

"No, I do not understand it," said Job. "The thunder of His power I shall never understand. But I believe that at least we are on the outskirts of His ways, and we shall hold on to that much."

Amy Carmichael shows different ways of struggling with problems that seem to have no answer.

He said, "I will forget the dying faces;
The empty places,
They shall be filled again.
O voices moaning deep within me, cease."
But vain the word; vain, vain:
Not in forgetting lieth peace.

He said, "I will withdraw me and be quiet,
Why meddle in life's riot?

HOW COME, GOD?

Shut be my door to pain.
Desire, thou dost befool me, thou shalt cease."
But vain the word; vain, vain:
Not in aloofness lieth peace.

He said, "I will accept the breaking sorrow
Which God tomorrow
Will to His son explain."
Then did the turmoil deep within him cease.
Not vain the word, not vain;
For in Acceptance lieth peace.[11]

[11]Amy Carmichael, *Toward Jerusalem.* London: Society for Promoting Christian Knowledge, 1936, pp. 40, 41.

IX

"When the Friendship of God Was Upon My Tent"

(Job, chs. 26, 27, 29-31)

We come now to Job's last discourse in Chapters 26 through 31. Chapter 26 is primarily an answer to Bildad, who had just given his final speech. Bildad touched on the sovereignty of God and Job began by amplifying this and speaking much more eloquently than Bildad.

Chapter 27 poses a textual problem. There is discussion among scholars as to the textual arrangement of Chapter 27. In the first six verses Job continued his protestation of innocence. But in verses 7 through 23 Job appears to be using the same argument that the friends had been making. He talked about how the wicked will be cut off and punished in this life. Some have suggested that this was really Zophar's final speech since Zophar does not speak a third time. I leave the textual problem to more competent scholars and pass on to Chapters 28 through 31.

Chapter 28 is Job's great discourse on wisdom. This has always been a bit of a problem to me. It does not seem to fit into the logical sequence of the rest of the book. It is hard to get the exact connection between the preceding arguments and what Job says in Chapter 28—unless you take Chapters 29 through 31 first. For the sake of clarity I will do this, as Chapter 28 makes far more sense in the light of Chapters 29 through 31.

In Chapter 29 Job referred to the glory of his former days.

And Job again took up his discourse, and said:

Oh, that I were as in the months of old,
 as in the days when God watched over me;
 when his lamp shone upon my head,
 and by his light I walked through darkness;
as I was in my autumn days,
 when the friendship of God was upon my tent (29:1–4).

In this time of great crisis, he was living in darkness, but he was looking back to the day when the presence of God was real to him, *"when the Almighty was yet with me"* (29:5a).

His family also had caused him joy in those days: *"when my children were about me"* (29:5b). Later, of course, his children were gone. His wife had forsaken him. He was alone in the world. He spoke out of a heart of terrible loneliness.

He remembered the prosperity he had,

When my steps were washed with milk,
 and the rock poured out for me streams of oil! (29:6).

Another factor that had contributed to his happiness was his prestige:

When I went out to the gate of the city,
 when I prepared my seat in the square,
the young men saw me and withdrew,
 and the aged rose and stood;
the princes refrained from talking,
 and laid their hand on their mouth;
the voice of the nobles was hushed,
 and their tongue cleaved to the roof of their mouth (29:7–10).

When Job appeared at the gate of the city, the younger men

stepped out of the way and the older men stood up as a sign of respect to him.

> *Men listened to me, and waited,*
> *and kept silence for my counsel.*
> *After I spoke they did not speak again,*
> *and my word dropped upon them.*
> *They waited for me as for the rain;*
> *and they opened their mouths as for the spring rain* (29:21–23).

Men used to anticipate his words. "They waited to hear what I had to say about things. Once I spoke, the rest of them kept quiet." This was the prestige that he had enjoyed. Now, having been spurned and despised by these same men, Job stood alone.

It is sad to see in complete loneliness a man who once enjoyed great prestige. I had such an experience a number of years ago in the airport in San José, Costa Rica. General Juan Perón, who had recently been deposed from the presidency of Argentina, was on the same plane. He was wandering around Latin America in exile before settling in Spain. On the plane no one paid him any attention. Finally, he stood up and walked back through the plane, just looking at people. I got the impression that he was hoping someone would show some sign of recognition. Here was a man at whose words people had bowed. The men stood up in the gates. The young men pulled out of the way, when Perón came by. But there he was, walking up the aisle of the plane with no one paying the least attention to him.

That night the plane was delayed about six hours for technical difficulties. It taxied back to the terminal where we disembarked and sat around the airport. A few people stepped up to speak to him and I had a short conversation with him. But I noticed as we went to get on the plane again that he was just like anyone else. No one stepped back to let him on first.

There was no particular fanfare for him. Everybody left him pretty much to himself. He must have been experiencing terrible loneliness as a man who once had enjoyed great prestige, completely ignored now as just one of the crowd.

Another source of happiness had been Job's outlet of serving other people.

> *. . . I delivered the poor who cried,*
> *and the fatherless who had none to help him. . . .*
> *I caused the widow's heart to sing for joy.*
>
> *I was eyes to the blind,*
> *and feet to the lame.*
> *I was a father to the poor,*
> *and I searched out the cause of him whom I did not know.*
> *I broke the fangs of the unrighteous,*
> *and made him drop his prey from his teeth* (29:12,13,15–17).

This was the joy that he had in helping people in need. He cared for the fatherless and the widows; he helped those who needed someone to stand up for them. Now his health was broken; his wealth was lost; his prestige was gone. There was no way for him to continue in this kind of service.

"I smiled on them when they had no confidence" (29:24). Job knew how to give a smile at just the right time to those who had lost confidence and needed a lift.

You have seen a little child get up before a school assembly or in a Sunday school program. Maybe it is his first time on the platform. He has learned his poem well. He recites the first line, and then it is gone. The poor child stands there, so frightened that his sense of self-confidence goes. He is about to burst into tears. Suddenly he catches sight of his teacher sitting on the front row, and she is smiling. Soon he breaks out in a beaming smile. He remembers again. His self-confidence returns. He recites his poem and the program is a success, because someone smiled on him when he lost his confidence.

Job had lost every one of these things. He no longer felt the presence of God. The friendship of God did not seem to be upon his tent. His family was gone. His prosperity was gone. His prestige was gone. His opportunity for social service was gone. His hope in the future was gone.

"Then I thought, 'I shall die in my nest' . . . " (29:18a). He had looked forward to being able to die peacefully in his home, having served his fellow men. But this kind of hope was gone too.

In Chapter 30 he described his present calamity.

> *But now they make sport of me,*
> *men who are younger than I. . . .*
>
> *They abhor me, they keep aloof from me;*
> *they do not hesitate to spit at the sight of me* (30:1,10).

When Job walked by, young men spit, just to show their disdain of him.

> *My heart is in turmoil, and is never still* (30:27a).

This was what he sensed, having lost all his former happiness.

What can be done about this? Job again protests that somehow these things did not fit in. That was what he had been before; this was what he was now. These were the facts. He was not arguing with the facts of the case. "But what is the reason?" said Job. He still had not found it.

In Chapter 31, he described his own righteousness. Eighteen different times in this chapter he used the word "if" in the form of a Hebrew oath which he invoked to claim his own innocence.

He claimed moral purity:

> *I have made a covenant with my eyes;*
> *how then could I look upon a virgin?* (31:1).

He maintained his truthfulness:

> *If I have walked with falsehood,*
>   *and my foot has hastened to deceit;*
> *(Let me be weighed in a just balance,*
>   *and let God know my integrity!)* (31:5, 6).

Job also invoked his concern for others:

> *If I have rejected the cause of my manservant or my maidservant,*
>   *when they brought a complaint against me;*
> *what then shall I do when God rises up?* (31:13, 14).

Job believed in racial and class equality. There was no class distinction between him and his servant. *"Did not he who made me in the womb make him?"* (31:15).

They had been his servants but he had been fair to them in every way.

> *If I have withheld anything that the poor desired,*
>   *or have caused the eyes of the widow to fail,*
> *or have eaten my morsel alone,*
>   *and the fatherless has not eaten of it* (31:16, 17)

—No Lazarus sat outside his gate, eating the crumbs that were thrown to the dog; he provided for those around him—

> *if I have seen anyone perish for lack of clothing,*
>   *or a poor man without covering; . . .*
> *and if he was not warmed with the fleece of my sheep; . . .*
> *then let my shoulder blade fall from my shoulder,*
>   *and let my arm be broken from its socket* (31:19, 20b, 22).

The hungry, the poor, those without clothing, all received help from Job. He provided shelter:

> *(The sojourner has not lodged in the street;*
>   *I have opened my doors to the wayfarer)* (31:32).

He was not an avaricious man looking for money:

> *If I have made gold my trust,*
>   *or called fine gold my confidence;*
> *if I have rejoiced because my wealth was great,*
>   *or because my hand had gotten much* (31:24,25)

—Gold was not his idol. Nor was he an idolatrous man in other ways—

> *if I have looked at the sun when it shone,*
> *or the moon moving in splendor* (31:26)

—There were sun worshipers in those days, and Job was claiming that he had not been among them—

> *and my heart has been secretly enticed,*
> *and my mouth has kissed my hand* (in worship of the sun, as it were);
> *this also would be an iniquity to be punished by the judges,*
> *for I should have been false to God above* (31:27,28).

He had not been vengeful against those who hated him nor had he cursed them.

> *If I have rejoiced at the ruin of him that hated me,*
> *or exulted when evil overtook him*
> *(I have not let my mouth sin*
> *by asking for his life with a curse)* . . . (31:29,30).

He could also claim openness and honesty:

> . . . *if I have concealed my transgressions from men,*
> *by hiding my iniquity in my bosom,* . . .
> *so that I kept silence, and did not go out of doors* . . . (31:33,34b).

He did not finish this sentence, but he was saying, "I have not hidden my iniquities or tried to cover things up. I have tried to be honest and open."

Having come to the end, he suddenly burst out with a great cry of anguish and agony, asking that God Himself would speak and show Job where he had been wrong.

> *Oh, that I had one to hear me!*
> *(Here is my signature! let the Almighty answer me!)*
> *Oh, that I had the indictment*
> *written by my adversary!* (31:35).

He was talking now in legal terms. An adversary had to bring a written document of accusation against the accused in court. So Job said, "If only my adversary would bring the written document and show me where I have actually been wrong. If this would come: *Surely I would carry it on my shoulder; I would bind it on me as a crown; I would give him an account of all my steps; like a prince I would approach him*" (31:36,37).

Job had a clean conscience. He could say, "If God Himself were to write out the accusation against me, I would still stand before Him as a prince." When Job's heart did not condemn him, he was on proper ground.

Job did not know it, but God had already said to Satan, "You write out an accusation against Job. He is a perfect man. Try to find something against him."

Job now had to find some kind of outlet. This is why Chapter 28 is more understandable at this point. Job had thought through these issues when he made his great proclamations about wisdom in Chapter 28. So let's listen now to his exposition of wisdom.

X

"Where Shall
Wisdom Be Found?"
(Job, ch. 28)

Having described his former greatness, his present calamity, and his own innocence, Job could not fit these things together. There was something missing. When human logic goes as far as it can and one fact is still missing, then is the time when God must step in.

Job came to this point. All the logic of man came up with no final explanation. So Job began to describe what man could and could not do. He started out by showing how man had been able to do great things.

> Surely there is a mine for silver,
>   and a place for gold which they refine.
> Iron is taken out of the earth,
>   and copper is smelted from the ore.
> Men put an end to darkness,
>   and search out to the farthest bound
>   the ore in gloom and deep darkness.
> They open shafts in a valley away from where men live;
>   they are forgotten by travelers,
>   they hang afar from men, they swing to and fro. . .

HOW COME, GOD?

Man puts his hand to the flinty rock,
and overturns mountains by the roots.
He cuts out channels in the rocks,
and his eye sees every precious thing.
He binds up the streams so that they do not trickle,
and the thing that is hid he brings forth to light (28:1–4,9–11).

"Man can do great things," said Job, "in cutting down into the depths of the earth and digging treasures."

But where shall wisdom be found? Now the problem begins. Man can do all these other things, but the logic of man cannot bring him to true wisdom. So Job asked the great question:

But where shall wisdom be found?
And where is the place of understanding?
Man does not know the way to it,

—he knows a lot of other things, but he does not know this—

and it is not found in the land of the living.
The deep says, "It is not in me,"
and the sea says, "It is not with me."
It cannot be gotten for gold,
and silver cannot be weighed as its price.
It cannot be valued in the gold of Ophir,
in precious onyx or sapphire. . . .

the price of wisdom is above pearls.
The topaz of Ethiopia cannot compare with it,
nor can it be valued in pure gold (28:12–16,18,19).

When it comes to the deep questions of real wisdom, man is at a loss. Where can wisdom be found? Man cannot find it. The earth cannot produce it. The sea does not know where it is.

Whence then comes wisdom?
And where is the place of understanding?
It is hid from the eyes of all living,
and concealed from the birds of the air.
Abaddon and Death say,
"We have heard a rumor of it with our ears" (28:20–22)

—but we don't know anything about it. We don't really know where it is.

Wisdom is basically a very practical thing. Webster defines it as "the ability to deal sagaciously with facts as they relate to life and conduct." In other words, wisdom has to work itself out in conduct.

Richardson's *Theological Word Book* defines it as "skill in making thought issue in the appropriate action."[12] Our ideas, our philosophy, our theology must issue in the appropriate action. So wisdom is not true wisdom unless it does this.

The New Bible Dictionary defines it as: "The art . . . of forming the correct plan to gain the desired results."[13] It is eminently practical and not theoretical. It is not limited to the realm of ideas. It is the ability to take ideas and put them into action.

Here is where Job ran into his problem. And this is why Chapter 28 is more understandable after Chapters 29 through 31. Job's problem was that in trying to put all the facts together he could not produce the right result. He had been an upright, honest, pure, and fair man. He did all the right things, and what happened? He ended up in the most disastrous condition.

These descriptions of Job are things that could have been said about two men with whom I have been closely associated. These things were some of the greatest characteristics of Kenneth Strachan. He was an honest and pure man, concerned for others, and was never unfair to those with whom he worked. Yet he died a painful death of incurable cancer.

---

[12] *A Theological Word Book of the Bible.* Edited by Alan Richardson. London: SCM Press Ltd. (1957), 1950, p. 282.

[13] *The New Bible Dictionary.* Edited by J. D. Douglas. Grand Rapids, Mich.: Wm. B. Eerdmans Publishing Co., 1962, p. 1333.

HOW COME, GOD?

Of all the men whom I have known well, few were more upright than Ernest Fowler. The better I got to know him, the more I saw the characteristics of Christ in his life. He was a fair man who loved other people and gave himself totally to them. Yet he died a violent death at the hands of murderous bandits in the high Andes of Colombia.

Can we put these things together? Man's wisdom cannot come up with the answer. This is what Job was grappling with. "Here are the facts," said Job. Wisdom is the ability to take those facts and put them together in such a way that one comes up with the right results. Job had not been able to do it, so he cried out, *"But where shall wisdom be found?* How am I going to get wisdom? If this is the way the facts of life are, if this is the way God treats us, where can wisdom be found? Man cannot find it. The sea cannot produce it. The living beings cannot produce it. It is not in the earth. It is not in the air. Where is it?"

> *God understands the way to it,*
>   *and he knows its place.*
> *For he looks to the ends of the earth,*
>   *and sees everything under the heavens.*
> *When he gave to the wind its weight,*
>   *and meted out the waters by measure;*
> *when he made a decree for the rain,*
>   *and a way for the lightning of the thunder;*
> *then he saw it and declared it;*
>   *he established it, and searched it out.*
> *And he said to man,*
> *"Behold, the fear of the Lord, that is wisdom;*
>   *and to depart from evil is understanding"* (28:23–28).

Job did not fully understand it, but he saw the Source of wisdom. He saw that while man cannot find wisdom in himself, and all the best reasoning of man cannot produce it, at least man can know where wisdom begins. *"Behold, the fear of the Lord, that is wisdom"* (28:28). Or, as Solomon said, *"The fear of the Lord is the beginning of wisdom"* (Prov. 9:10).

A personal letter to me spoke of suffering in this way:

> .... the collapse of the Roman Empire (when Christians along with patricians were chopped to bits by the Huns and Goths); or like the English Civil War when Christians on both sides were ground to mincemeat; or like the French Revolution, when again no one, be his faith never so robust, was exempt from the tribulation.
>
> We were reading Psalm 46 the other night. ("Therefore will not we fear, though the earth be removed . . . God shall help her, and that right early. . . . The Lord of hosts is with us.") Godly people in every era have read this and been chopped to bits with the rest of the populace. Which is to say simply that, whatever form that divine help may take, it is not to be expected that it implies exemption from participation in whatever the suffering is that the world is being asked to sustain. The immediate response to the eye of non-faith is, of course, "He trusted in God that he would deliver him, let Him deliver him." Jesus believed that and got done in anyway. At least, so it appeared. But faith insists that, oddly enough, God *did* deliver him, and that his faith was not misconceived; that there is a sense which does not at all appear to the eye of mere logic, far more true and real than the ephemeral actualities of crucifixion or fire and sword, in which God *is* our refuge and strength. Not a womb. Not an escape pass. Not twelve legions of angels. But in some radically real sense, a refuge.[14]

The problem is to find that radically real sense in which God is a refuge. It cannot mean that in every case a Christian will be delivered physically by God. If so, how come Ernest Fowler lies buried today up in the mountains of Colombia? There must be some other way to put these facts together.

Here is what Job was struggling with. Wisdom has to take the facts and somehow put them together in a way that will

---

[14]Personal letter from Thomas Howard, February 21, 1968.

produce results. And man cannot do it. So Job came to his great conclusion: wisdom is found only with God.

> *God understands the way to it,*
> *and he knows its place* (28:23).

"The fear of the Lord," expressed in a godly walk and in fellowship with the Father, is the true basis of wisdom. Whatever the sufferings, whatever the incomprehensible tragedies of life, whatever the darkness that encompasses us, the man who walks in fellowship with God is the man who has found true wisdom. And this is the only reward that can be claimed.

XI

"When He Is Quiet, Who Can Condemn?"
(Elihu, chs. 32-35)

Throughout the long exchanges between Job and his friends, one young man, Elihu, had sat quietly listening. The other three friends differ very little from each other in discussing the problems of Job, but Elihu has some flashes of originality. His discourse begins in Chapter 32, where the introduction gives the background for what he had to say.

> So these three men ceased to answer Job, because he was righteous in his own eyes. Then Elihu the son of Barachel the Buzite, of the family of Ram, became angry. He was angry at Job because he justified himself rather than God; he was angry also at Job's three friends because they had found no answer, although they had declared Job to be in the wrong. Now Elihu had waited to speak to Job because they were older than he. And when Elihu saw that there was no answer in the mouth of these three men, he became angry (32:1-5).

Four times the introduction refers to Elihu being angry. The basic motivation at this point seems to be his own anger. There is nothing wrong with this if the anger is based on the right things. He was angry at Job because Job continually justified himself. Elihu stood with the friends on this point. He did not believe that Job was as innocent as he claimed to be. On the other hand, he was equally angry at the three friends who, while they condemned Job, had no adequate answers for him. On this point he was right. They had found it all too easy to condemn him without coming up with an answer.

So Elihu began to speak:

> *I am young in years,*
> *and you are aged;*
> *therefore I was timid and afraid*
> *to declare my opinion to you.*
> *I said, "Let days speak,*
> *and many years teach wisdom"* (32:6,7).

He was hoping that sooner or later one of these older men, who had more wisdom than he, would come through with an adequate solution. Having listened patiently to this long debate, he concluded that none of these men was right.

> *But it is the spirit in a man,*
> *the breath of the Almighty, that makes him understand.*
> *It is not the old that are wise,*
> *nor the aged that understand what is right.*
> *Therefore I say, "Listen to me;*
> *let me also declare my opinion"* (32:8–10).

He claimed that age is not the only factor in knowledge. Here again he was right. God can reveal to a young man, just as well as to an old man, some adequate answers.

I have learned from younger Christians in Colombia some of the greatest lessons of my life. Nothing has been more enjoyable than sitting on a log in the woods with a man who perhaps had just come to know the Lord recently and hearing him talk about the Word of God. Frequently these men think that they are learning from me. But the very questions they ask reveal a lot about the Word of God and I have come to realize along with Elihu, that the breath of the Almighty is what makes a man understand.

Throughout history students have frequently been in the vanguard of intellectual and spiritual advance. Dr. Clarence Shedd of Yale University wrote in 1943:

> In all ages the great creative religious ideas have been the achievement of the intellectual and spiritual insight of young men. . . . In literature, the arts, the sciences, many of the most revolutionary ideas have been worked out by young men under thirty and frequently by youth between eighteen and twenty-five. . . . Since Jesus' time numberless bands of Christian youth have turned the world upside down and thus led mankind forward in its struggle for freedom and deeper religious experience.[15]

Elihu felt that although he was young, God was saying something to him and he had to pass it on. There was an inner constraint to speak.

> *They are discomfited, they answer no more;*
> *they have not a word to say.*
> *And shall I wait, because they do not speak,*
> *because they stand there, and answer no more?*
> *I also will give my answer;*
> *I also will declare my opinion.*
> *For I am full of words,*
> *the spirit within me constrains me.*
> *Behold, my heart is like wine that has no vent;*
> *like new wineskins, it is ready to burst.*
> *I must speak, that I may find relief;*
> *I must open my lips and answer* (32:15–20).

Elihu could hardly wait to speak, because he had something to say.

[15]Clarence P. Shedd, *Two Centuries of Student Christian Movements.* New York: Association Press, 1943 p. 1

HOW COME, GOD?

Years ago my two younger brothers got into an argument at the table. The youngest, Jim, who was about four years old, was chattering on and on, dominating the conversation. Finally, Tom, who was a few years older but still quite young at the time, burst out with great exasperation and said, "Jim, for goodness' sake, why do you talk all the time?" Jim's very simple and straightforward answer was, "Because I have so much to say."

That may be an adequate reason for talking as long as what a man has to say is worth saying. There are times, however, when one has a perfect right to feel like Elihu and say that he must speak to find relief.

Victor Landero of Colombia once told me that when he first became a Christian he would often go to bed at night with a hoarse voice from talking to people all day about the Lord. Then he moved up the San Jorge River to the village of Puerto Libertador with the purpose of evangelizing that area. He recalls those days as follows: "In the first six days that I was in Puerto Libertador, I could find no one with whom to have a natural contact to talk about the Lord. Can you imagine that I actually went for six whole days without witnessing to one person about Christ? I thought I would burst!"

He had sat quietly, but he really did have something to say, and he was now ready to burst.

Elihu claimed equality with Job before God.

> The spirit of God has made me,
>   and the breath of the Almighty gives me life. . . .
> Behold, I am toward God as you are;
>   I too was formed from a piece of clay (33:4,6).

Then Elihu began talking about God's different ways of dealing with men. Here he grasped a real truth. Having summarized what Job said—in verse 9:

> *You say, "I am clean, without transgressions;*
> *I am pure, and there is no iniquity in me . . . "*

—he went on in verse 12:

> *Behold, in this you are not right. I will answer you.*
>   *God is greater than man.*
> *Why do you contend against him,*
>   *saying, "He will answer none of my words"?*
> *For God speaks in one way,*
>   *and in two, though man does not perceive it* (33:12–14).

He then mentioned two different ways in which God speaks. Elihu was not saying that these are the only ways that God speaks, but he was saying that there are different ways and here are two of them. First:

> *In a dream, in a vision of the night,*
>   *when deep sleep falls upon men,*
>   *while they slumber on their beds,*
> *then he opens the ears of men,*
>   *and terrifies them with warnings,*
> *that he may turn man aside from his deed,*
>   *and cut off pride from man* (33:15–17).

Sometimes, Elihu said, God uses a dream to convict a man of his sin, to bring him back into the right relationship with God. God did this on more than one occasion in Scripture.

We may think that today God would not do this. However, I cannot deny that God works through dreams, because I have seen the results of it.

One day I was walking through the woods in Colombia with a good friend named Adán Ricardo. I asked him to tell me how he became a Christian. He was a leader in the church of which he was a member and for a period of time he was the layworker in charge of that church. That very morning I had baptized his twelve-year-old son.

He said, "I cannot read. So I could not come to know the Lord through reading the Bible. I would never listen to anybody who would talk to me about Christ. Victor Landero tried to evangelize me and I turned my back on him. One night I had a dream. In my dream I was walking down the road. Jesus Christ came toward me, stopped me, and said, 'Adán, you are a sinner and you need Me.' I turned my back on Him and woke up. I tried to forget about the dream.

"The next night I had the same dream again. I was walking down the road. Christ came along in the opposite direction. He stopped me and said, "Adán Ricardo, you are a sinner and you need Me. I am the only hope you have.' I could turn away from Victor Landero. But I could not turn away from Jesus Christ. When I woke up that night, I got down on my knees and received Him into my heart—and that's how I came to know Him."

How could I deny that this was true? I know from the fruit of his life that he is a man of God. As Elihu said, God may speak through a dream.

Elihu went on to say that God has another method through which He speaks. This is a point which had not yet come up, but Elihu perceived it.

> *Man is also chastened with pain upon his bed,*
> *and with continual strife in his bones;*
> *so that his life loathes bread,*
> *and his appetite dainty food* (33:19,20).

This almost seems to be a description of Job. Elihu was saying that God sometimes chooses to speak to a man through pain.

Then what will He do in the midst of pain? Sometimes in God's mercy He will send a special messenger to help the man interpret the pain.

> *If there be for him an angel,*
> *a mediator* [or "interpreter"], *one of the thousand,*

> *to declare to man what is right for him;*
> *and he is gracious to him* . . . (33:23,24).

Sometimes God sends this special interpreter who can help us understand what He is saying to us.

What will the result be if the person responds properly?

> *Then man prays to God, and he accepts him,*
> *he comes into his presence with joy.*
> *He recounts to men his salvation* (33:26).

The man who had been at the gates of despair, God, through an interpreter, brings back into His presence with joy. There is spiritual renewal. The result is that he wants to share this with others.

> *. . . and he sings before men, and says:*
> *"I sinned, and perverted what was right,*
> *and it was not requited to me.*
> *He has redeemed my soul from going down into the Pit,*
> *and my life shall see the light"* (33:27,28).

Thus Elihu declared that God has different ways of speaking, but in each of those ways we must be ready to listen and to respond.

Elihu went on in Chapter 34 to summarize Job's argument:

> *For Job has said, "I am innocent,*
> *and God has taken away my right;*
> *in spite of my right I am counted a liar;*
> *my wound is incurable, though I am without transgression"*
> (34:5,6).

This is a fair summary of much of what Job had said. He summarized further in one other statement:

> *For he has said, "It profits a man nothing*
> *that he should take delight in God"* (34:9).

This is nearly a direct quotation from Job who had said, in the midst of deep depression,

HOW COME, GOD?

What is the Almighty, that we should serve him?
And what profit do we get if we pray to him? (21:15).

Moffatt translates this verse, ". . . it is no use for man to be the friend of God." Elihu said that this was Job's contention. Elihu was getting down to the heart of the problem in a way that the other friends never did. He understands that the real problem is not so much the question of innocent suffering as it is the problem of whether or not it is worth it to trust God. Do we trust Him for naught? Or, do we trust the Lord regardless of outward profit?

This is a crucial issue in this book. Satan tried to claim this to God at the beginning. He sneered, "Of course Job is going to trust you. But take away everything he has and see what happens." So God said, "Go ahead." And Satan did. Yet Job did not curse God. Then God asked, "How about it now?" And Satan said, "All right, a man will give everything for his life. Touch his body and see what happens." When Satan touched his body, the battle began—between a man who was trusting God regardless of the outward circumstances and Satan who was trying to break down that faith by saying, "You see, it doesn't do any good to trust God."

Elihu quoted Job properly when he claimed, "You've said it profits a man nothing that he should take delight in God." But Job was not saying only this. Elihu had not understood all of what Job was saying. In the midst of his despair, Job still held on to God even though in the dark.

Elihu summarized these two arguments of Job—his claim of innocence and his claim that it does not profit to trust God. Next he tried to refute the arguments by pointing out that God has absolute authority and justice:

> . . . far be it from God that he should do wickedness,
> and from the Almighty that he should do wrong.

> *For according to the work of a man he will requite him,*
> *and according to his ways he will make it befall him.*
> *Of a truth, God will not do wickedly,*
> *and the Almighty will not pervert justice* (34:10–12).

It seemed that Job was accusing God of perverting justice. Elihu countered that He would not do this.

> *Who gave him charge over the earth*
> *and who laid on him the whole world?* (34:13).

Elihu here grasped another great truth: the absolute authority of God. Nobody gave Him His authority. He has it by His own nature.

> *If he should take back his spirit to himself,*
> *and gather to himself his breath,*
> *all flesh would perish together,*
> *and man would return to dust* (34:14,15).

If God let go of things, there would be nothing left.

Job and his friends were struggling with the problem: where was God in the midst of this? Elihu declared that one thing was certain, if God let go, then everything would perish, because God was holding things together.

He then spoke about the omniscience and the omnipotence of God:

> *For his eyes are upon the ways of a man,*
> *and he sees all his steps.*
> *There is no gloom or deep darkness*
> *where evildoers may hide themselves . . .* (34:21,22).

> *When he is quiet, who can condemn?*
> *When he hides his face, who can behold him,*
> *whether it be a nation or a man?* (34:29).

In that last phrase Elihu moved from the general to the specific. Whether it be a whole nation that is trying to find God or whether it be one man like Job, it makes no difference.

HOW COME, GOD?

God is omnipotent. When He hides His face, who can behold Him? Elihu emphasized the authority, the justice, and the sovereignty of God.

In Chapter 35 he answered Job's second complaint, quoting him: *"What advantage have I? How am I better off than if I had sinned?"* (35:3). Job was saying, "Even if I had sinned, what difference would it have made? I did not sin and I am suffering like this, so what is the difference? " Elihu answered him:

> *But none says, "where is God my Maker,*
>   *who gives songs in the night,*
> *who teaches us more than the beasts of the earth,*
>   *and makes us wiser than the birds of the air?"*
> *There they cry out, but he does not answer,*
>   *because of the pride of evil men.*
> *Surely God does not hear an empty cry,*
>   *nor does the Almighty regard it* (35:10–13).

Elihu claimed that there *was* a difference when a man sinned. God will not hear the empty cry of an evil man, but He certainly hears the cry of a godly man, even when it seems as though He is not heeding it.

XII

"For Love, He Causes It to Happen"
(Elihu, chs. 36, 37)

Next Elihu moved into a great discourse on the mighty works of God found in all spheres of life. In Chapter 36 we find the key to all that Elihu was saying.

He began by apologizing for being long-winded:

> *Bear with me a little, and I will show you,*
> *for I have yet something to say on God's behalf.*
> *I will fetch my knowledge from afar,*
> *and ascribe righteousness to my Maker* (36:2,3).

Then he exalts the justice of God.

> *Behold, God is mighty, and does not despise any;*
> *he is mighty in strength of understanding.*
> *He does not keep the wicked alive,*
> *but gives the afflicted their right.*
> *He does not withdraw his eyes from the righteous* (36:5–7).

Verse 15 contains a key to Elihu's arguments: *"He delivers the afflicted"*—not from their affliction, but—*"by their affliction, and opens their ear by adversity."* In the use of His sovereign rights, God sometimes delivers and teaches a man in the midst of adversity and affliction. This is a point that the other friends never understood. The only thing the other friends could see about suffering was that it had to be the result of sin. Elihu saw it from another angle. He brought out a truth not yet touched upon—that suffering may be God's means of teaching a man, rather than of punishing him.

This is the great difference between Elihu and the other friends. They could believe only that suffering had to be God's means of punishment. Elihu saw that suffering may be God's means of teaching. And so he said, *"He delivers the afflicted"*—not necessarily physically, but He delivers them —*"by their affliction."*

> *Behold, God is exalted in his power;*
> *who is a teacher like him?* (36:22).

Who would have thought of affliction as a means of teaching? This is not the way we would choose to be taught. But sometimes this is God's way.

> *Who has prescribed for him his way,*
> *or who can say, "Thou hast done wrong"?* (36:23).

Who can tell God He has done wrong when He tries to teach a man through affliction? God may be delivering him into something far greater in his relationship with God than he ever could have had before.

In a darkened room near Lancaster, Pa., lies an elderly Chinese lady, a converted Buddhist named Christiana Tsai. For more than forty years Miss Tsai has been unable to see the light due to a strange malady which has affected her eyesight. Her body has been wracked with pain and crippled by disease which has kept her bedridden for all those years. Yet in the midst of indescribable suffering she has been a shining light of testimony to the grace of God. Hundreds have been led to Christ at her bedside. Thousands around the world have been drawn to God through her autobiography entitled *Queen of the Dark Chamber,* which has gone into dozens of editions in numerous languages.[16] Countless others have been touched by her prayers. I have had the privilege of entering her darkened chamber and immediately sensing the presence of God. To hear her talk of the goodness of the Lord, and then to be the object of her prayers as she pours out her heart to the One she loves on behalf of her friends, is an unforgettable experience. But without the long years of suffering her far-reaching ministry would not have developed. She has learned, with Elihu, that God may use affliction as a teacher to draw us to Himself.

Then Elihu extolled God as the great creator:

Behold, God is great, and we know him not;
  the number of his years is unsearchable (36:26).

Then he listed five different aspects of God's moving in the midst of nature. He spoke first of rain.

For he draws up the drops of water,
  he distils his mist in rain
which the skies pour down,
  and drop upon man abundantly (36:27,28).

From 36:29 to 37:5 he talked about thunder and lightning.

He covers his hands with the lightning,
  and commands it to strike the mark.
Its crashing declares concerning him,
  who is jealous with anger against iniquity. . . .

Hearken to the thunder of his voice
  and the rumbling that comes from his mouth.
Under the whole heaven he lets it go,
  and his lightning to the corners of the earth.

---

[16]Christiana Tsai, *Queen of the Dark Chamber.* Chicago: Moody Press, 1966.

HOW COME, GOD?

> *After it his voice roars;*
> *he thunders with his majestic voice*
> *and he does not restrain the lightnings when his voice is heard.*
> *God thunders wondrously with his voice;*
> *he does great things which we cannot comprehend*
> (36:32,33; 37:2–5).

Even in nature God does things we cannot understand. How can man understand and explain the lightning and the thunder? God does great things beyond our understanding, just as He does in the area of affliction and pain. In the midst of thunder and lightning in nature God is carrying out His own purpose.

Next he talked about the snow:

> *For to the snow he says, "Fall on the earth";*
> *and to the shower and the rain, "Be strong"* (37:6).

He talked about ice:

> *By the breath of God ice is given,*
> *and the broad waters are frozen fast* (37:10).

Then he spoke of the clouds:

> *He loads the thick cloud with moisture;*
> *the clouds scatter his lightning.*
> *They turn round and round by his guidance,*
> *to accomplish all that he commands them*
> *on the face of the habitable world* (37:11,12).

Elihu claims that the clouds are actually carrying out God's purposes. God guides the clouds around the heavens as part of His purposes.

Verse 13 is a great commentary on weather. What is the reason for God's working in the snow, the ice, the rain, the clouds?

> *Whether for correction, or for his land,*
> *or for love, he causes it to happen* (37:13).

It may be *"for correction"*; that is, God will send the elements against mankind to punish them. He did it once in the flood, according to His own Word. He did it again in some of the plagues in Egypt. He may do it at other times.

It may be *"for his land."* God sends the rain for the use of the land. His land needs the moisture that comes through snow and rain.

But what about this: *"or for love"*? Can the weather be a result of God's love? Why did God make snow? In addition to the good it does to the land, can it be because God, who loves beauty, wants us to enjoy beauty? The New Testament says that God has given us all things richly to enjoy. That includes snow. We could get along without snow as long as we had rain, but snow is beautiful and God sends it for us to enjoy.

Why does God send ice? Have you ever looked out after an ice storm? How beautiful the crystal designs of the leaves and the trees covered with ice! The God who loves beauty rejoices in covering His countryside with the incomparable jewels of ice.

The weather itself is a part of God's love for us. Elihu grasped a facet of truth here. God may send weather for correction; He may send it to keep the land going; and it may be because He loves us and wants us to enjoy these things.

So Elihu came to his great conclusion in the final verses of Chapter 37.

> *Hear this, O Job;*
> *stop and consider the wondrous works of God.*
> *Do you know how God lays his command upon them,*
> *and causes the lightning of his cloud to shine?*
> *Do you know the balancings of the clouds,*
> *the wondrous works of him who is perfect in knowledge,*
> *you whose garments are hot*
> *when the earth is still because of the south wind?*

HOW COME, GOD?

> *Can you, like him, spread out the skies,*
> *hard as a molten mirror?*
> *Teach us what we shall say to him;*
> *we cannot draw up our case because of darkness* (37:14–19).

We shall never be able to make a case against God because of darkness. It is useless to argue with God. So, in his conclusion, he pointed out that our knowledge is limited. Some things we do know. But in the final analysis there is darkness for us; we do not know.

> *And now men cannot look on the light*
> *when it is bright in the skies,*
> *when the wind has passed and cleared them.*
> *Out of the north comes golden splendor;*
> *God is clothed with terrible majesty* (37:21,22).

Having spoken on the one hand about darkness, next he spoke about the brightness of God. God is so bright that no man can look upon Him. We cannot look into the sun and take in its beauty. Our eyes are not made for that. We would have to have a special kind of glasses to look into the sun and see what is there. Nor can we look on God in all of His splendor and majesty and expect to understand Him completely. It takes special eyes of revelation from God to see this.

> *The Almighty—we cannot find him;*
> *he is great in power and justice,*
> *and abundant righteousness he will not violate* (37:23).

Moffatt translates this, "The Almighty is beyond our minds." We shall never understand some things about God until God in His mercy reveals them to us. Thus, as Elihu came to his discourse, he brought some new segments of truth to the argument, particularly this—that God in the midst of adversity is teaching men about Himself. Suffering can be God's channel for disciplinary teaching as well as disciplinary punishment. God is too dark—and too bright—for us to understand fully.

Thomas Binney, the hymn writer, expressed it this way:

Eternal Light! Eternal Light!
  How pure the soul must be,
When, placed within Thy searching light,
It shrinks not, but with calm delight
  Can live, and look on Thee!

The spirits that surround Thy throne
  May bear the burning bliss;
But that is surely theirs alone,
Since they have never, never known
  A fallen world like this.

O, how shall I, whose native sphere
  Is dark, whose mind is dim,
Before the Ineffable appear,
And on my naked spirit bear
  The uncreated beam?

There is a way for man to rise
  To that sublime abode;
An offering and a sacrifice,
A Holy Spirit's energies,
  An advocate with God:

These, these prepare us for the sight
  Of holiness above;
The sons of ignorance and night
May dwell in the eternal Light,
  Through the eternal Love.

XIII

"Where Were You...?"
(Jehovah ,chs. 38-41)

As we come to the great discourse of God, it will be well to review the position of the five previous speakers.

First, there was the problem that Job faced, which was his basic relationship to God. Job was suffering physically, intellectually, emotionally, and spiritually, as he struggled with this issue.

Eliphaz, who has been described as the pious mystic, believed that suffering is the direct result of sin. He limited everything to his own experience. He said, "Job, this is the way we have seen it and you have to fit into this." Job's experience did not fit into what Eliphaz had seen. So Eliphaz failed.

Bildad has been described as the traditionalist. "Job, this is the way it has always been. God has to continue working in your life the way He has worked in the lives of others that we have known." He based his arguments on tradition which was not sufficient to answer Job's need.

Zophar was the dogmatist. He attacked Job more directly

than anyone else. He told Job he was getting less than he deserved. But his words did not reach the heart of Job or meet his need.

Elihu took a different approach and came up with more truth than the others. He saw that suffering may be a channel of God's teaching for man. But even this did not help Job to face the situation.

So finally the Lord had to speak. Even more important, in one sense, than what He said is the very fact that He *did* speak. The silence of God is broken. The voice out of the whirlwind assures Job and his friends that the God of the universe has heard their debate and is now revealing Himself to them in a personal way. The Lord of all creation is interested in individual man and his problems. He came to make personal contact with the man who had been looking for Him.

> *Then the Lord answered Job out of the whirlwind:*
> *Who is this that darkens counsel by words without knowledge?*
> *Gird up your loins like a man,*
> *I will question you, and you shall declare to me* (38:1–3).

Here the Lord used an interesting word for "man." He did not use the most common word but rather one which refers to man in his strength. It is similar to the concept of *machismo* in Spanish. It speaks of man in all of his strength as a combatant who stands up and fights. Job had been pleading for this. He said, "Oh, I wish I could stand up and fight. I wish I knew where my enemy was. I wish I knew what I was fighting with." So God said, "All right, now gird up your loins like a man; stand up and fight and listen to what I have to say."

> *Where were you when I laid the foundation of the earth?*
> *Tell me, if you have understanding.*
> *Who determined its measurements—surely you know!*
> *Or who stretched the line upon it?*

HOW COME, GOD?

> *On what were its bases sunk,*
> *or who laid its cornerstone,*
> *when the morning stars sang together,*
> *and all the sons of God shouted for joy?* (38:4–7).

Then God began to describe different aspects of nature:

> *Or who shut in the sea with doors,*
> *when it burst forth from the womb . . . ?* (38:8).

He spoke of the morning, and dawn.

> *Have you commanded the morning since your days began,*
> *and caused the dawn to know its place. . . .*
>
> *Where is the way to the dwelling of light,*
> *and where is the place of darkness,*
> *that you may take it to its territory*
> *and that you may discern the paths to its home?* (38:12,19,20).

Notice the irony in verse 21:

> *You know, for you were born then,*
> *and the number of your days is great!*

Then He spoke of the snow, rain, and ice.

> *Have you entered the storehouses of the snow,*
> *or have you seen the storehouses of the hail . . . ?*
>
> *Who has cleft a channel for the torrents of rain,*
> *and a way for the thunderbolt . . . ?*
>
> *Has the rain a father,*
> *or who has begotten the drops of dew?*
> *From whose womb did the ice come forth,*
> *and who has given birth to the hoarfrost of heaven?*
> (38:22,25,28,29).

He spoke of the stars:

> *Can you bind the chains of the Pleiades,*
> *or loose the cords of Orion?*

> *Can you lead forth the Mazzaroth in their season,*
> *or can you guide the Bear with its children?* (38:31,32).

And the clouds—

> *Can you lift up your voice to the clouds,*
> *that a flood of waters may cover you?*
> *Can you send forth lightnings, that they may go*
> *and say to you, "Here we are"?*
> *Who has put wisdom in the clouds,*
> *or given understanding to the mists?* (38:34–36).

Then, having spoken of all these elements of nature—the sea, the morning, the dawn, the snow, rain, and ice, He began to speak of the animals:

> *Can you hunt the prey for the lion,*
> *or satisfy the appetite of the young lions,*
> *when they crouch in their dens,*
> *or lie in wait in their covert?*
> *Who provides for the raven its prey,*
> *when its young ones cry to God,*
> *and wander about for lack of food?*
> *Do you know when the mountain goats bring forth?*
> *Do you observe the calving of the hinds?* (38:39–39:1).
>
> *Who has let the wild ass go free?*
> *Who has loosed the bonds of the swift ass . . . ?* (39:5).
>
> *Is the wild ox willing to serve you?*
> *Will he spend the night at your crib?* (39:9).
>
> *The wings of the ostrich wave proudly;*
> *but are they the pinions and plumage of love?* (39:13).
>
> *Do you give the horse his might?*
> *Do you clothe his neck with strength?*
> *Do you make him leap like the locust?* (39:19,20a).
>
> *Is it by your wisdom that the hawk soars,*
> *and spreads his wings toward the south?*
> *Is it at your command that the eagle mounts up*
> *and makes his nest on high?* (39:26,27).

105

HOW COME, GOD?

Then God summarized by saying,

> *Shall a faultfinder contend with the Almighty?*
> *He who argues with God, let him answer it* (40:2).

Job could not begin to answer this description of all the wisdom of God in nature. What did he know about the morning? What did he know about the movement of the stars? What did he know about the strength of the horse, the hawk, the eagle?

Job tried to interrupt hoping that the Lord would stop, because he had had enough. He said, *"Behold, I am of small account; what shall I answer thee?"* (40:4a). Job had not yet come to the point of admitting sin. Rather he recognized his insignificance. The phrase "of small account" has no moral overtones. It suggests, "I am insignificant in the light of this. I don't count for anything."

This is where God had placed him. This was God's purpose. Job was forced to say:

> *Behold, I am of small account; what shall I answer thee?*
> *I lay my hand on my mouth.*
> *I have spoken once, and I will not answer:*
> *twice, but I will proceed no further* (40:4,5).

Job was through, but the Lord was not. He continued:

> *Gird up your loins like a man;*
> *I will question you, and you declare to me.*
> *Will you even put me in the wrong?*
> *Will you condemn me that you may be justified?* (40:7,8).

Although he never did it directly, Job had come perilously close to condemning God to justify himself. So God called him on it. How easy it is for a man to condemn God in order to justify his own position!

Then God moved into a description of two great monsters—Behemoth and Leviathan. Some believe this refers back to the Babylonian stories of the pre-creation chaotic condition with the struggle between light and darkness. Others believe it is a representation of the power of darkness. Some scholars agree on Behemoth as a description of the hippopotamus and Leviathan as a description of the crocodile. Whatever the exact interpretation may be, God was giving here a picture of an awesomely powerful creation of His, which only He could control.

> *Behold, Behemoth,*
> *which I made as I made you;*
> *he eats grass like an ox.*
> *Behold, his strength in his loins,*
> *and his power in the muscles of his belly.*
> *He makes his tail stiff like a cedar;*
> *the sinews of his thighs are knit together.*
> *His bones are tubes of bronze,*
> *his limbs like bars of iron.*
> *He is the first of the works of God . . .*
>
> *Can one take him with hooks,*
> *or pierce his nose with a snare?* (40:15–19,24).

Then He described Leviathan, which may well be the crocodile.

> *Can you draw out Leviathan with a fishhook,*
> *or press down his tongue with a cord?*
> *Can you put a rope in his nose,*
> *or pierce his jaw with a hook?*
> *Will he make many supplications to you?*
> *Will he speak to you soft words?* (41:1–3).

What could man do in the face of creatures like this? Man could not control that kind of power. God was emphasizing to Job His wisdom and His unlimited power. What could Job say?

XIV

"Now My Eye Sees Thee"
(Epilogue, ch. 42)

By the opening of Chapter 42 God had taken Job out of the center of the picture. Up to this point, Job had put himself in the place where the world was revolving around him. The more he talked, the more he moved himself into the center of the universe.

God quickly removed him from there and put him where he had to confess his own insignificance and the greatness of God.

> *I know that thou canst do all things,*
> *and that no purpose of thine can be thwarted* (42:2).

He quoted what God had said about him:

> *"Who is this that hides counsel without knowledge?"*
> *Therefore I have uttered what I did not understand,*
> *things too wonderful for me, which I did not know* (42:3).

He recognized that he had said things he did not fully understand and had no right to say. Then he begins his confession.

> *I had heard of thee by the hearing of the ear,*
> *but now my eye sees thee* (42:5).

108

Job said, "I had heard about all these things, but I had never had a face-to-face encounter with God. Now, suddenly, through this act of suffering and through all the arguments that go with it, I see You with my eye. Therefore . . ."

> . . . *I despise myself,*
> *and repent in dust and ashes* (42:6).

The word used here for "despise" means "repudiate"—"I recognize now that I cannot come face to face with God and still maintain my own righteousness. I repudiate myself and repent in dust and ashes."

Job had no other way to come except the way of repentance. He was forced into it by God. It is significant that nowhere in God's speeches did He answer Job's questions! He did not talk about suffering. All the things that these men had discussed were not even mentioned by God. Instead of answering the questions they had debated, God overwhelms them with *more* questions!

The overpowering presence of God in His creation utterly dwarfs the questions which Job and his friends had raised. They are bludgeoned into silence by the towering majesty of God. No explanations are given to the problem of suffering. There is silence on the issues so hotly debated throughout the book. Yet the need of Job's heart is met. The full extent of human logic and wisdom pales into insignificance as the infinite power of a mighty God and the eternal mercy of a loving Father reach out to His confused yet searching child. Job now sees Him in a personal way, and his only answer is to submit in worship, confession, and gratitude.

Now God turned to Eliphaz as the main spokesman for the friends: *"My wrath is kindled against you and against your two friends; for you have not spoken of me what is right, as my servant Job has"* (42:7). Some of the things they had said about

God were true. But they did not get the whole picture. Job came closer to the truth than they did. Four times He used the phrase "My servant Job," in verses 7 and 8 of Chapter 42:

> *Now therefore take seven bulls and seven rams, and go to*
> *my servant Job, and offer up for yourselves a burnt offering;*
> *and my servant Job shall pray for you, for I will accept his*
> *prayer not to deal with you according to your folly; for you*
> *have not spoken of me what is right, as my servant Job has* (42:8).

God vindicated Job in the sight of his friends. "Job is *my* servant. Even when you accuse him of blasphemy, he is *my* servant. This is the man who is going to pray for you now."

God's vindication of Job, who had raised serious doubts about the reality and presence of God in his life, is in striking contrast to the harsh words God reserves for the friends. It indicates that God is more pleased with daring honesty, even when this involves doubt about God and His ways with man, than He is with a superficial attempt to maintain a shallow creed in the face of shattering evidence. It was Job who expressed doubts. The friends never ventured outside the bounds of their creed. They dared not raise the great questions that Job raised.

But for Job, this creed had long since been destroyed. There was nothing left of his understanding of God as he had known Him before. This had all been shattered, and Job openly and honestly stated this:

Tennyson, in his great poem "In Memoriam," describes a doubter. Perhaps he had Job in mind when he wrote:

> *You tell me, doubt is Devil born.*
>
> *I know not; one indeed I knew*
> *In many a subtle question versed,*
> *Who touch'd a jarring lyre at first,*
> *But ever strove to make it true:*

Perplext in faith, but pure in deeds,
   At last he beat his music out.
   There lives more faith in honest doubt,
Believe me, than in half the creeds.

He fought his doubts and gather'd strength,
   He would not make his judgment blind,
   He faced the spectres of the mind
And laid them: thus he came at length

To find a stronger faith his own;
   And Power was with him in the night,
   Which makes the darkness and the light,
And dwells not in the light alone,

But in the darkness and the cloud
   As over Sinai's peaks of old,
   While Israel made their gods of gold,
Altho' the trumpet blew so loud. [17]

There is the picture of Job—a man who expressed his doubts and fought them. He came through in the midst of darkness and God poured out His light upon him at the end. There was more truth in those honest doubts of Job than in all the creeds of his friends.

Job prayed for his friends:

> . . . *and the Lord accepted Job's prayer. And the Lord restored the fortunes of Job, when he had prayed for his friends . . .*
> (42:9b,10a).

It is significant that God responds to the physical and material needs of Job when Job takes an interest in the spiritual needs of his friends. This must have been a difficult prayer for Job. He was not yet healed physically. He was still desolate and stripped of his material goods. His family was gone. His friends had heaped ridicule and rebuke upon him. Now, even

[17]Alfred Tennyson. *op. cit.*, p. 312.

before the healing light breaks through, he is being asked by God to pray for these men who had treated him with contempt in the midst of his agony. And Job obeys.

> *. . . and the Lord gave Job twice as much as he had before* (42:10b).

God will never betray the man who accepts Him in repentance and who reaches out in love and mercy to his fellow men, as Job did.

> *And the Lord blessed the latter days of Job more than his beginning;*
> *and he had fourteen thousand sheep, six thousand camels,*
> *a thousand yoke of oxen, and a thousand she-asses. He had also seven*
> *sons and three daughters . . . And in all the land there were no*
> *women so fair as Job's daughters* (42:12–13,15a).

Not only did God give him double what he had before, but God added special physical beauty to the lovely daughters that were to grace his household. This was the icing on the cake. All through Job's long night of distress no promise is given that there will be a rosy dawn to follow. God wants Job to respond in faith regardless of physical and material matters. And when Job does respond in faith, God answers with an abundant outpouring of blessing that Job never could have dreamed of.

* * * * * * * * * *

In conclusion, let's summarize a few lessons.

First, suffering is a part of God's design. God had to show this somewhere in the Old Testament, so that the people of God in the New Testament would be prepared for God, through suffering, to bring redemption to mankind. Margaret Clarkson, of Toronto, has written a poem based on Ps. 119:75, that expresses this truth.

> *I know, O Lord, that thy judgments are right and that in faithfulness*
> *thou hast afflicted me.*

In faithfulness hast Thou afflicted me,
  O Sovereign Love;
I will not fear, but look in faith to Thee
  Enthroned above;
And know my Father's heart of grace has planned
This darkness that I cannot understand.

I rest in Thee, though human tears may fall
  In sorrow's hour;
Upon Thy faithfulness I cast my all,
  And claim Thy power
To work eternal wealth of holy gain
From this deep night of loneliness and pain.

In faithfulness hast Thou afflicted me,
  Most gracious One;
In faithfulness may I accept from Thee
  This Thou hast done;
For Thou Thy gifts of darkness dost impart
But to disclose the fullness of Thy heart.

Second, experience cannot be the only basis of faith in God because experience is too limited. This was the problem with Job's friends. Their experience was not great enough to encompass the fullness of God. They had only a limited picture of who God is.

Third, God must be God. We cannot place God in a box of our own making. No definition ever given of God has been fully satisfactory. God must be God in the fullest meaning of that word.

> [Job] realizes that his concept of God collapsed because it was too small; his problems evaporate when he realizes the greatness of God. The book does not set out to answer the problems of suffering but to proclaim a God so great that no answer is needed, for it would transcend the finite mind if given.[18]

[18] *The New Bible Dictionary*, p. 637.

HOW COME, GOD?

No real answer is given in this book to the problem raised. God Himself is so great that if an answer were given, we could not understand it. It goes beyond the finiteness of human minds and brings us to our knees with Job.

It is of God's grace that Job has had a foretaste and so became a pioneer to those to whom the Spirit still says: "Behold, I stand at the door and knock." . . . If after reading the Book of Job we ask "Where do we go from here?" we must answer: to the foot of the Cross and beyond in the company of the risen Lord. . . . The reality of religion, to which Job bears witness in anticipation, lies in the Everlasting Mercy.

> 'Tis mystery all! The immortal dies!
> Who can explore His strange design!
> In vain the first-born seraph tries
> To sound the depths of love divine:
> 'Tis mercy all! Let earth adore,
> Let angel-minds inquire no more.
> —*Charles Wesley*[19]

[19]Edgar Jones, *The Triumph of Job.* London: SCM Press Ltd., 1966, pp. 118, 119.

XV

And After This Job Lived. . . ."
(Conclusion)

Recently I heard Norman Grubb, a true elder statesman of missions and of the joyful Christian life, give his testimony. He spoke of the years of World War I when he went through personal struggles in his relationship to God. He told of entering Cambridge University following the war, where he was used of God, along with fellow students, to give cohesion and direction to the student witness which was to grow into the movement known as Inter-Varsity Fellowship. But doubts and struggles were not absent from his Christian experience. In speaking of them he said with a delightful twinkle in his eye, "The only decent way to faith is through doubt. If you are going to have a good dose of faith, you have to have a good dose of doubt." And for more than half a century Norman Grubb, who had his doubts, has been a man of towering faith.

And so it was with Job. Having come out of the long tunnel of darkness, he burst into the light of new-found faith and joy, a faith which, we can safely assume, never left him.

"And after this Job lived a hundred and forty years, and saw his sons, and his sons' sons, four generations. (42:16)"

Those must have been happy years, as Job watched his family grow. What a privilege those children and grandchildren for four generations must have had! Imagine sitting on the knee of hoary-headed Job as he recounted his adventures with God! His understanding of the valley of the shadow of death had to be deeper than that of any man of his time (or perhaps of all history). So when we read *"and after this Job lived . . ."* what a life it must have been!

Several days after the death of Dale Bowman, described in Chapter I, Ron Kernaghan came to my cabin in Camp Roblealto late at night. He was disturbed and needed to share his thoughts with someone. Ron was a man who almost literally had returned from the dead. In his forty-five minutes of terrible struggle against the tide and waves in attempting to save Dale, he had come to the conclusion that there was no hope. But he determined that he would never leave Dale. So he resigned himself to die.

As he faced what to him was certain death, he had two reactions. First, he was angry with God, because he didn't want to die. In less than a month Ron was to be married, and he resented the thought that now he would never experience the joy of marriage with the one he loved. Second, he had an overwhelming sense of the presence of God, even in the face of imminent death.

Now Ron had returned from the dead, and he felt like a man who wasn't supposed to be alive. He belonged beyond the watery grave with Dale. But God had chosen for him to live. Life now took on new meaning for Ron. As with Job, who had felt that he really belonged in the grave, and who even wished that he had never been born, it could now be said, "And Ron LIVED. . . ."

Ron has since shared with me that this experience of death has convinced him of the stewardship of life. Life, in a very special way for him, is a gift from God, and he wants to live it out for God. He no longer fears death, for he knows what true life is.

Those final one hundred and forty years of Job's long life must have been years when he demonstrated in a remarkable way what it is to LIVE. Life, in all of its fullness and beauty, was his. It was to be savored, to be used in true stewardship, to be shared with others, and to be the pathway to final reunion with God. The long road leading up to the Celestial City must have become brighter and brighter. As with Bunyan's Pilgrim, so with Job. The sight of the towers of that city must have evoked new praise and shouts of joy. Life was coming to its fruition and blossoming out into all the fullness of eternal life.

And Job died, an old man, and full of days (42:17).

The Septuagint adds a beautiful postscript to this verse with the reading,

> *And it is written that he will rise again*
> *with those whom the Lord raises up.*

While this may not be a part of the original text, it is a fitting and true commentary on this man who lived through darkness, doubt, and despair, who returned to live life in all of its fullness, and who finished his course with joy.

> *Long the blessed guide has led me, by the desert road;*
> *Now I see the golden towers, City of my God.*
> *There amidst the love and glory He is waiting yet;*
> *On His hands a name is graven He can ne'er forget.*
>
> *O the blessed joy of meeting, all the desert past,*
> *O the wondrous words of greeting He shall speak at last!*
> *He and I together ent'ring those fair courts above;*
> *He and I together sharing all the Father's love.*
>
> *He who in His hour of sorrow bore the curse alone;*
> *I who through the lonely desert trod where He had gone;*
> *He and I, in that bright glory, one deep joy shall share—*
> *Mine, to be forever with Him; His, that I am there.*

117

Date Due
